The Regional Salmon Outmigration Study—Survival and Migration Routing of Juvenile Chinook Salmon in the Sacramento-San Joaquin River Delta during the Winter of 2008–09

By Jason G. Romine, Russell W. Perry, Scott J. Brewer, Noah S. Adams, Theresa L. Liedtke, Aaron R. Blake, and Jon R. Burau

Prepared in cooperation with the California Department of Water Resources and Bureau of Reclamation

Open-File Report 2013-1142

U.S. Department of the Interior
U.S. Geological Survey

U.S. Department of the Interior
SALLY JEWELL, Secretary

U.S. Geological Survey
Suzette M. Kimball, Acting Director

U.S. Geological Survey, Reston, Virginia: 2013

For product and ordering information:
World Wide Web: http://www.usgs.gov/pubprod
Telephone: 1-888-ASK-USGS

For an overview of USGS information products, including maps, imagery, and publications,
visit http://www.usgs.gov/pubprod

To order this and other USGS information products, visit http://store.usgs.gov

Suggested citation:
Romine, J.G., Perry, R.W., Brewer, S.J., Adams, N.S., Liedtke, T.L., Blake, A.R., and Burau, J.R., 2013,
The Regional Salmon Outmigration Study—Survival and migration routing of juvenile Chinook salmon in
the Sacramento-San Joaquin River Delta during the winter of 2008–09: U.S. Geological Survey Open-
File Report 2013-1142, 36 p.

Contents

Figures

Tables

Conversion Factors and Datums

Conversion Factors

Inch/Pound to SI

Multiply	By	To obtain
Length		
foot (ft)	0.3048	meter (m)
Flow rate		
foot per second (ft/s)	0.3048	meter per second (m/s)
cubic foot per second (ft^3/s)	0.02832	cubic meter per second (m^3/s)

SI to Inch/Pound

Multiply	By	To obtain
Length		
millimeter (mm)	0.03937	inch (in.)
kilometer (km)	0.6214	Mile (mi)
Volume		
liter (L)	33.82	ounce, fluid (fl. oz)
Mass		
gram (g)	0.03527	ounce, avoirdupois (oz)

Temperature in degrees Celsius (°C) may be converted to degrees Fahrenheit (°F) as follows:°F=(1.8×°C)+32. Concentrations of chemical constituents in water are given either in milligrams per liter (mg/L).

Datums

Horizontal coordinate information is referenced to North American Datum of 1983 (NAD 83).

The Regional Salmon Outmigration Study—Survival and Migration Routing of Juvenile Chinook Salmon in the Sacramento-San Joaquin River Delta during the Winter of 2008–09

By Jason G. Romine, Russell W. Perry, Scott J. Brewer, Noah S. Adams, Theresa L. Liedtke, Aaron R. Blake, and Jon R. Burau

Abstract

Juvenile Chinook salmon (*Oncorhynchus tshawytscha*) emigrating from natal tributaries of the Sacramento River may use a number of migration routes to navigate the Sacramento-San Joaquin River Delta (hereafter called "the Delta"), each of which may influence their probability of surviving. We applied a mark-recapture model to data from acoustically tagged juvenile late fall-run Chinook salmon that migrated through the Delta during the winter of 2008–09 to estimate route entrainment, survival, and migration times through the Delta.

A tag-life study was conducted to determine the potential for premature tag failure. Tag failure began after 12 days and continued until the 45th day. Travel times of tagged fish exceeded minimum tag-failure times, indicating that survival estimates obtained from this study were negatively biased due to tag failure prior to fish exiting the Delta. Survival estimates were not adjusted and represent the joint probability of tag survival and fish survival. However, relative comparisons of survival among Chinook salmon choosing different routes appeared to be robust to tag failure, and migration-routing parameters were unaffected by tag failure.

Migration-routing patterns were consistent among release groups. The Sacramento River was the primary migration route for all release groups except one. The percentage of fish entering the Sacramento River ranged from 33 to 55 percent. Sutter and Steamboat Sloughs were the secondary migration route for 9 of the 10 releases. The percentage of fish migrating through this route ranged from 10 to 35 percent. Entrainment into the interior Delta ranged from 15 to 33 percent. The Delta Cross Channel gates were open for 7 of the 10 releases. Entrainment into the interior Delta through the cross channel ranged from 1 to 27 percent.

We estimated route-specific survival for 10 release groups that were released between November 14, 2008, and January 19, 2009. Population-level survival through the Delta (S_{Delta}) ranged from 0.019 (standard error of 0.012) to 0.277 (standard error of 0.041) among releases, which represent the probability of a fish surviving from Sacramento to Chipps Island with an operational transmitter. Sacramento River flows throughout the study period were approximately 8,000–15,000 cubic feet per second at Freeport, suggesting that variability in flow contributed little to differences in survival between releases. Fish migrating through the Sacramento River had the highest survival for most releases. Survival in Sutter and Steamboat Sloughs was slightly lower than survival in the Sacramento River for 7 of the 10 releases, but higher than survival in the Sacramento River for 3 releases. Survival in the interior Delta was lowest for all release groups except for one release in November. With the exception of this November release, survival patterns across release groups were similar to those of previous studies.

Introduction

Many stocks of Chinook salmon (*Oncorhynchus tshawytscha*) in California, Washington, and Oregon are listed as threatened or endangered under the Endangered Species Act (Nehlsen and others, 1991; Myers and others, 1998). In the Central Valley of California, the winter, spring, and fall-late fall runs of Chinook salmon are federally listed as endangered, threatened, and "species of concern," respectively (National Marine Fisheries Service, 1997). Recently, owing to below-target returns of fall Chinook salmon to the Sacramento River, the National Marine Fisheries Service declared a Federal Disaster and closed the 2008 salmon fishery along the West Coast (National Oceanic and Atmospheric Administration, 2008). Understanding factors affecting survival of salmon is critical to developing effective recovery strategies for these populations.

An important stage in the life history of Chinook salmon is the period of migration from natal tributaries to the ocean, when mortality of juvenile salmon in the Sacramento River may increase as a result of various anthropogenic and natural factors (Baker and Morhardt, 2001; Brandes and McLain, 2001; Williams, 2006). Juvenile Chinook salmon emigrating from the Sacramento River must pass through the Sacramento-San Joaquin River Delta (hereafter called "the Delta", fig. 1), a complex network of natural and man-made river channels linking the Sacramento River with San Francisco Bay (Nichols and others, 1986). Juvenile salmon may migrate through a number of routes on their journey to the ocean—for example, they may migrate within the main stem Sacramento River leading directly into San Francisco Bay (see Route A in fig. 1). However, juvenile salmon also may migrate through longer secondary routes such as the interior Delta, the network of channels to the south of the main stem Sacramento River (see Routes C and D in fig. 1). Juvenile salmon entering the interior Delta also are exposed to entrainment at water pumping projects in the southern Delta, which may decrease survival of fish using this migratory pathway (Kjelson and others, 1981; Brandes and McLain, 2001; Newman and Rice, 2002; Newman, 2003; Kimmerer, 2008; Newman, 2008; Newman and Brandes, 2010; Perry and others, 2010, 2012a).

There is limited understanding of how water management actions in the Delta affect the population distribution and the route-specific survival of juvenile salmon during their outmigration. To address these uncertainties, we developed a mark-recapture model similar to that of Perry and others (2010) to estimate the route-specific components of population-level survival for acoustically tagged, late fall-run Chinook smolts migrating through the Delta. This study provided the first quantitative estimates of route-specific survival through the Delta, and of the fraction of the population that uses each migration route. Furthermore, we explicitly quantified the relative contribution of each migration route to population-level survival. As with other authors (Newman and Brandes, 2010), we found that survival of fish migrating through the interior Delta was lower than survival of fish migrating through the Sacramento River. The proportion of the population entering the interior Delta differed between releases, which can influence population-level survival by shifting a fraction of the population from a low-survival migration route (the interior Delta) to a high-survival route (the Sacramento River). However, differences in population-level survival between releases were caused by changes in survival for given migration routes. These findings indicated that variation in population-level survival was driven by variation in movement among routes and survival within routes.

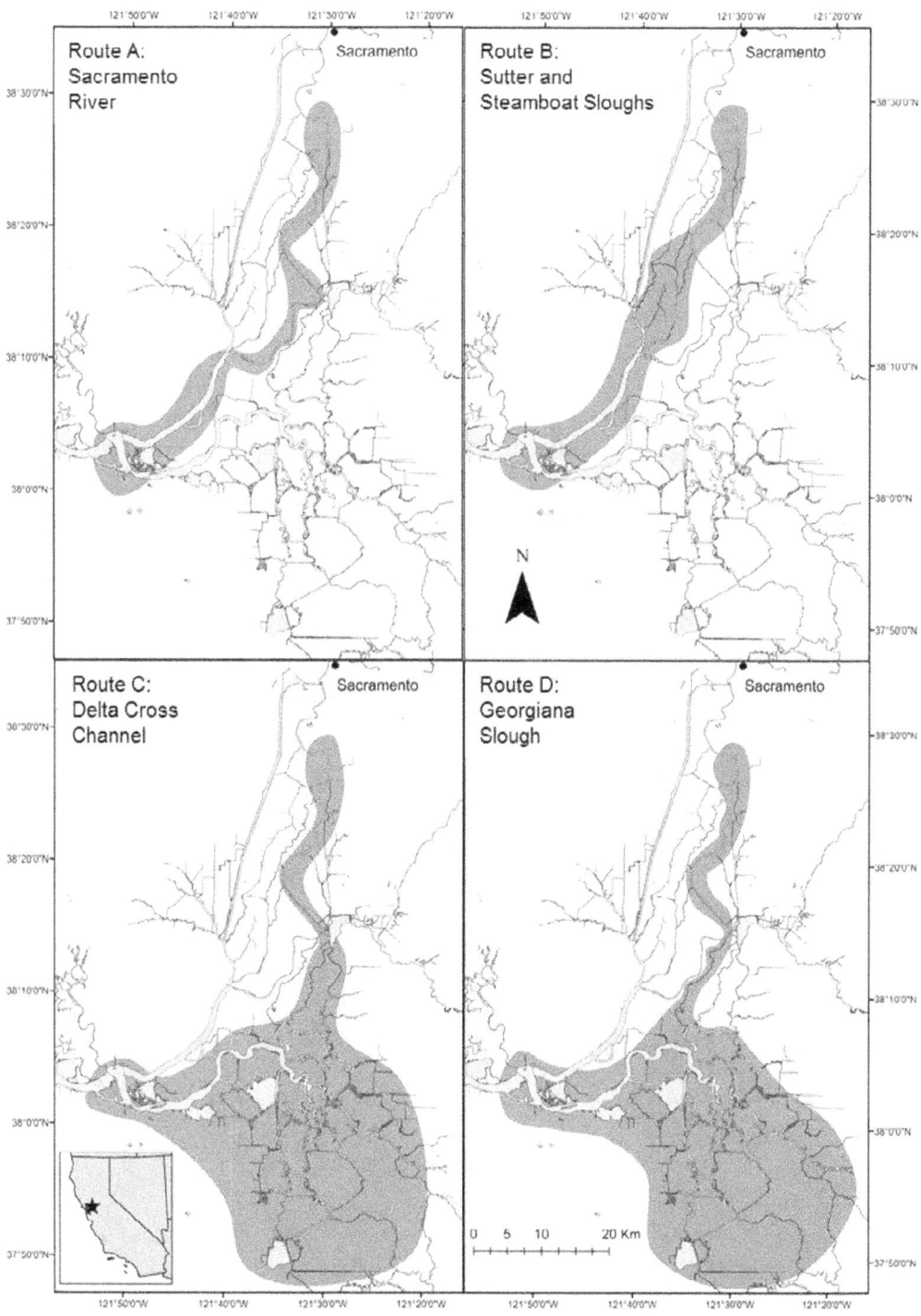

Figure 1. Maps showing the Sacramento-San Joaquin River Delta, California, with shaded regions showing river reaches that constitute Chinook salmon survival through the Delta for four different migration routes. For routes C and D, the interior Delta is the large shaded region in the southernmost part of the migration route. Base map provided by Bureau of Reclamation, Mid-Pacific Region, MPGIS Service Center, Sacramento, CA.

This report is the result of efforts by California Department of Water Resources and the Bureau of Reclamation to resume analysis of data collected during the 2008 Regional Salmon Outmigration Study. For the complete scope of the Regional Salmon Outmigration study, see the independent review of the study plan (Calfed Bay-Delta Program, 2012). The 2008 study was affected by a complete stop-work order in early 2009 because of the fiscal crisis in California. The analysis of survival that we present is only one aspect of the much larger and more ambitious study plan. Because survival was not the only factor driving the study design (e.g., 2-d behavior at river junctions), last-minute decisions made prior to implementation of the field work negatively impacted our ability to obtain unbiased estimates of survival. Early in the planning process, we anticipated that a 30-d tag life was necessary to estimate survival without bias, which could be achieved by manipulating the parameters (code length and period) of the signal emitted by the tag to extend its functional battery life. However, after compiling and reviewing tag-life data from recently completed studies in the Columbia River that had used the same tag, we determined that it was impossible to obtain a 30-d tag life. We considered using a relatively new tag that could meet our tag-life requirements, but it had not been used in large quantities, and we were concerned that early-run production issues might affect the reliability of the new tag. At the time of this decision, the outmigration season was nearly upon us so we moved forward with the existing tag knowing that tag life would be about one-half (14–18 d) of what we thought was needed to meet the survival objectives. In anticipation of reduced tag life, we added additional releases of tagged fish at Ryde and Georgiana Slough, which are located about halfway through the study area. In theory, this would effectively achieve the 30-d tag life by using Sacramento-released fish to estimate survival to Ryde and Georgiana Slough, and then using the fish released at Ryde and Georgiana Slough to estimate survival to Chipps Island. Even with these contingencies in place, longer than anticipated travel times exceeded tag life. The decision was made to proceed with the study despite the uncertainty of meeting the survival objectives because other objectives of the larger study plan could be met. Specifically, we were able to gather previously unattainable information about route selection, migration behavior, and travel time, and detailed information on the behavior of fish at critical junctions (Delta Cross Channel and Georgiana Slough) in the Delta. This information is critical for developing strategies to manage water conveyance in the Delta, while contributing to the recovery of threatened and endangered salmon populations.

Methods

Telemetry System

Telemetry stations were deployed to monitor the movement of tagged fish among four major migration routes through the Delta (fig. 1)—the main stem Sacramento River (Route A), Steamboat and Sutter Sloughs (Route B), the interior Delta through the Delta Cross Channel (Route C), and the interior Delta through Georgiana Slough (Route D; fig. 1). Telemetry stations were labeled hierarchically to reflect the branching nature of channels at river junctions and their subsequent downstream convergence at the confluence of river channels (fig. 2). Each telemetry station consisted of a single node or multiple nodes (Hydroacoustic Technology Incorporated (HTI), Seattle, Washington) that identified individual fish based on pulse rate from a transmitter or tag. Because the Sacramento River is the primary migration route, the ith telemetry station within this route was denoted as A_i from the release site to the last telemetry station in the Delta at Chipps Island (A_5). Sutter and Steamboat Sloughs (labeled B_i) diverge from the Sacramento River at the first river junction and converge again with the Sacramento River upstream of A_4. Dual telemetry arrays were deployed at the entrances to Sutter and Steamboat Sloughs to quantify survival and movement within this region. The dual arrays allowed independent estimation of detection probabilities at these locations. The entrance to Sutter Slough was labeled B_{11} and the entrance to Steamboat Slough was labeled B_{21} (fig. 2). The interior Delta consisted of Routes C and D. The entrance to the interior Delta through Georgiana Slough was labeled as D_1. Data from telemetry stations in the lower Mokelumne River and lower Potato Slough were pooled to form D_2. The entrance to the interior Delta through the Delta Cross Channel was labeled as C_1 where it diverges from the Sacramento River at the second river junction. Data from telemetry stations at the heads of the North and South Forks of the Mokelumne River were pooled to form station C_2. Following this hierarchy, routes A, B, C, and D contained 4, 3, 2, and 2 telemetry stations, respectively. We used a total of 12 telemetry stations to estimate survival. Parameter subscripting and coding of detection histories followed this hierarchical structure (see section, "Model Development").

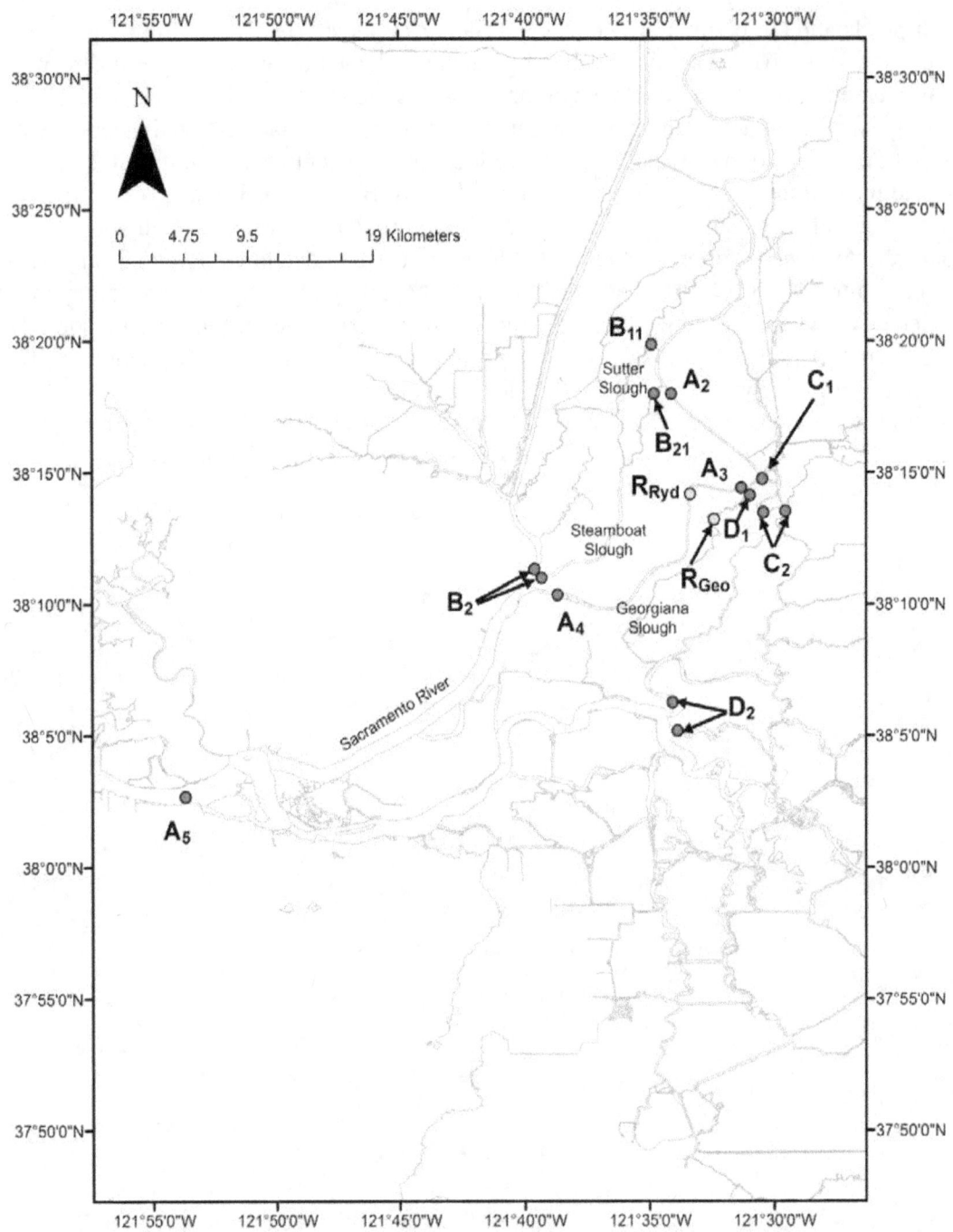

Figure 2. Map showing location of telemetry stations used to estimate survival and migration route probabilities within four major migration routes of the Sacramento-San Joaquin River Delta, California, during the winter of 2008–09. Red-filled circles labeled as h_i show the location of telemetry station i with route h (h = A, B, C, or D). The Sacramento (Tower Bridge) release site was 40 river kilometers upstream of station A_2. The Georgiana and Ryde release sites are noted as the green-filled circles labeled as R_{Geo} and R_{Ryd}, respectively. Base map provided by Bureau of Reclamation, Mid-Pacific Region, MPGIS Service Center, Sacramento, CA.

Fish Tagging and Release

Juvenile late fall-run Chinook salmon were obtained from the Coleman National Fish Hatchery (about 340 river kilometers upstream of the Tower Bridge near Sacramento). Fish were surgically implanted with a 1.6-g tag with a 12-d expected battery life (HTI, Model 795-E). Between November 14, 2008, and January 19, 2009, 10 releases were made across 3 separate sites (table 1). For each release group, fish were released at Sacramento (Tower Bridge), Ryde, and Georgiana Slough (fig. 2, table 1). Multiple release sites were used because of the 12-d battery life of the transmitters. For the Sacramento release site, transmitters were expected to stop transmitting before fish from the uppermost release site exited the Delta at Chipps Island. Therefore, the two downstream release sites (i.e., Ryde and Georgiana Slough) were used in an effort to obtain unbiased survival estimates in the lower regions of the Delta. Releases were made approximately every 2–3 d during this time period. For each release, fish were released first at Sacramento, and then released 1–2 d later at the downstream release locations, Ryde and Georgiana Slough. This was done to accommodate travel times of fish from the upper Sacramento to the lower release sites.

Untagged fish were transported from the hatchery to release sites where transmitters were implanted. Except for a minimum size criteria of 29.5 g, fish were randomly selected for tagging, resulting in a mean fork length (FL) of 149.9 mm (standard deviation =7.24) and mean weight of 38.4 g (SD=6.00). Tag burden ranged from 0.022 to 0.054 and averaged 0.042 (SD=0.006). Fish were collected 21 times from November 9, 2008, to January 17, 2009, and were transported in 265-L insulated tanks at a density of no greater than 20 g of fish per L of water. Water in transport tanks was maintained at 80–130 percent oxygen saturation using bottled oxygen. At each tagging site (Sacramento, Ryde, and Georgiana Slough), transport tanks were supplied with circulated fresh river water for 18–36 h prior to tagging. Fish were considered suitable for tagging if they were free of major injuries, had no external signs of gas bubble trauma, were less than 20-percent descaled, and had no other abnormalities.

To implant the transmitters, fish were anesthetized using buffered tricane® methanosulfate (MS-222) at a dosage of between 70 and 90 mg/L. After a fish lost equilibrium, it was removed from the anesthetic bucket, placed in a bin containing river water and Stress Coat® (Aquarium Pharmaceuticals, Inc.), weighed to the nearest 0.1 g, and measured to the nearest millimeter (FL). After a fish was anesthetized, a small incision was made in the abdomen between the pectoral fins and the pelvic girdle. The transmitter was inserted in to the peritoneal cavity, and the incision was closed with two interrupted sutures (4-0 nylon sutures with FS-2 cutting needle). Immediately following the tagging procedure, each fish was placed in a 19-L recovery bucket filled with 7–10 L of fresh river water and supplied with bottled oxygen (at 120–150 percent dissolved oxygen saturation) for at least 10 minutes. Each recovery bucket held a maximum of four surgically tagged, late fall-run Chinook salmon. After a minimum of 10 minutes, buckets were poured into 121-L plastic drums that mostly were submerged in the river. These drums were perforated to allow water circulation and were placed inside a polyvinyl chloride frame for flotation to ensure fish had access to the water surface.

Table 1. Summary of release dates, locations, and sample size of acoustically tagged late fall-run Chinook salmon released into the Sacramento-San Joaquin River Delta, California, during the winter of 2008–09.

Release Date	Release No.	Release Location	Sample Size
November 14-15, 2008	1	Sacramento	164
November 16-17, 2008	1	Ryde (Sacramento)	69
November 16-17, 2008	1	Georgiana Slough	101
November 17-18, 2008	2	Sacramento	179
November 19-20, 2008	2	Ryde (Sacramento)	69
November 19-20, 2008	2	Georgiana Slough	103
November 30- December 1 2008	3	Sacramento	177
December 2-3, 2008	3	Ryde (Sacramento)	61
December 2-3, 2008	3	Georgiana Slough	95
December 3-4, 2008	4	Sacramento	182
December 5-6, 2008	4	Ryde (Sacramento)	77
December 5-6, 2008	4	Georgiana Slough	137
December 14-15, 2008	5	Sacramento	191
December 16-17, 2008	5	Ryde (Sacramento)	69
December 16-17, 2008	5	Georgiana Slough	108
December 17-18, 2008	6	Sacramento	179
December 19-20, 2008	6	Ryde (Sacramento)	69
December 19-20, 2008	6	Georgiana Slough	108
December 30-31, 2008	7	Sacramento	175
January 1-2, 2009	7	Ryde (Sacramento)	69
January 1-2, 2009	7	Georgiana Slough	108
January 2-3, 2009	8	Sacramento	177
January 4-5, 2009	8	Ryde (Sacramento)	69
January 4-5, 2009	8	Georgiana Slough	109
January 13-14, 2009	9	Sacramento	177
January 14-16, 2009	9	Ryde (Sacramento)	69
January 15-16, 2009	9	Georgiana Slough	107
January 16-17, 2009	10	Sacramento	178
January 17-18, 2009	10	Ryde (Sacramento)	69
January 18-19, 2009	10	Georgiana Slough	106

Tag Life

A tag-life study was conducted to estimate the battery-life distribution and to determine if survival estimates could be negatively biased due to tag failure prior to fish exiting the system. The study was conducted at the U. S. Geological Survey Columbia River Research Laboratory (CRRL). Tags used in the tag-life study were identical to those implanted in fish. A total of 148 795-E tags (HTI) were activated and placed in a circular 5-ft diameter tank with constantly flowing water. Tags emitted a constant double-pulse every 3–10 s with a pulse width of 1ms depending on tag programming. Tags were monitored with two model 290 HTI hydrophones to determine when tags ceased operating.

Water temperature was controlled to match the daily mean (1999–2008) water temperature in the Sacramento River at the Rio Vista (RIV) gaging station (California Department of Water Resources, 2013). Tank water temperature was monitored using a digital thermometer and recorded every 30 minutes by two Onset® tidbit® data loggers.

Tag-life time was calculated as the elapsed time between tag activation and the time of last detection recorded by the hydrophones. A Kaplan-Meier tag-life curve then was fitted to the data using the R statistical package (R Development Core Team, 2011). Cumulative travel time distributions for each release location and reach then were plotted against the tag-life curve. This allowed us to assess whether tagged fish exited the study area before tags began failing.

Model Development

We used a survival model similar to the model presented in Perry and Skalski (2010). In this model, we estimated detection (P_{hi}), survival (S_{hi}), and route entrainment probabilities (Ψ_{hl}). Detection probabilities (P_{hi}) estimate the probability of detecting a transmitter assuming a fish is alive and the transmitter operational at telemetry station i within route h (h=A, B, C, D; fig. 2). Survival probabilities (S_{hi}) estimate the probability of surviving from telemetry station i to i+1 within route h (that is, to the next downstream telemetry station), conditional on surviving to station i (figs. 2 and 3). Route entrainment probabilities (Ψ_{hl}) estimate the probability of a fish entering route h at junction l (l=1, 2), conditional on fish migrating through junction l (figs. 2 and 3).

Dual telemetry stations within Sutter and Steamboat Sloughs downstream of each entrance allowed us to estimate route entrainment probabilities separately for each slough (figs. 2 and 3). The parameter Ψ_{B11} estimates the probability of being entrained into Sutter Slough at station B_{11}, and Ψ_{B21} estimates the probability of being entrained into Steamboat Slough at station B_{21}. Because route entrainment probabilities must sum to one at a given river junction, $1-\Psi_{B11}-\Psi_{B21} = \Psi_{A1}$ is the probability of remaining in the Sacramento River at the first junction (figs. 2 and 3). The second junction was modeled as a three-branch junction where Ψ_{A2}, Ψ_{C2}, and $1-\Psi_{A2}-\Psi_{C2} = \Psi_{D2}$ estimate the probabilities of remaining in the Sacramento River (Route A), being entrained into the Delta Cross Channel (Route C), and entering Georgiana Slough (Route D) at junction 2 (figs. 2 and 3). The Delta Cross Channel gates were opened at about 8:45 a.m. and closed at 3:45 p.m. daily from November 14 to December 22, 2008, after which they were closed for the remainder of the study. Fish released during this time period passed the junction when gates were both open and closed. After the December 22, 2008 closure of the gates, they were not opened for the remainder of the study period; thus, fish released after this date could not enter the Delta Cross Channel. Therefore, we incorporated a parameter to estimate the probability of fish passing this river junction when the gates were open (ω_{open}, fig. 3). We then estimated route entrainment probabilities conditional on gate position (i.e., $\Psi_{hl,\text{open}}$ and $\Psi_{hl,\text{closed}}$). Route-specific survival was estimated for each release group. For the first seven release groups, route-specific survival represents the average survival during conditions experienced by each release-group; that is, with the Delta Cross Channel gates both open and closed. Route-specific survival for subsequent release groups represents survival when the gates were closed.

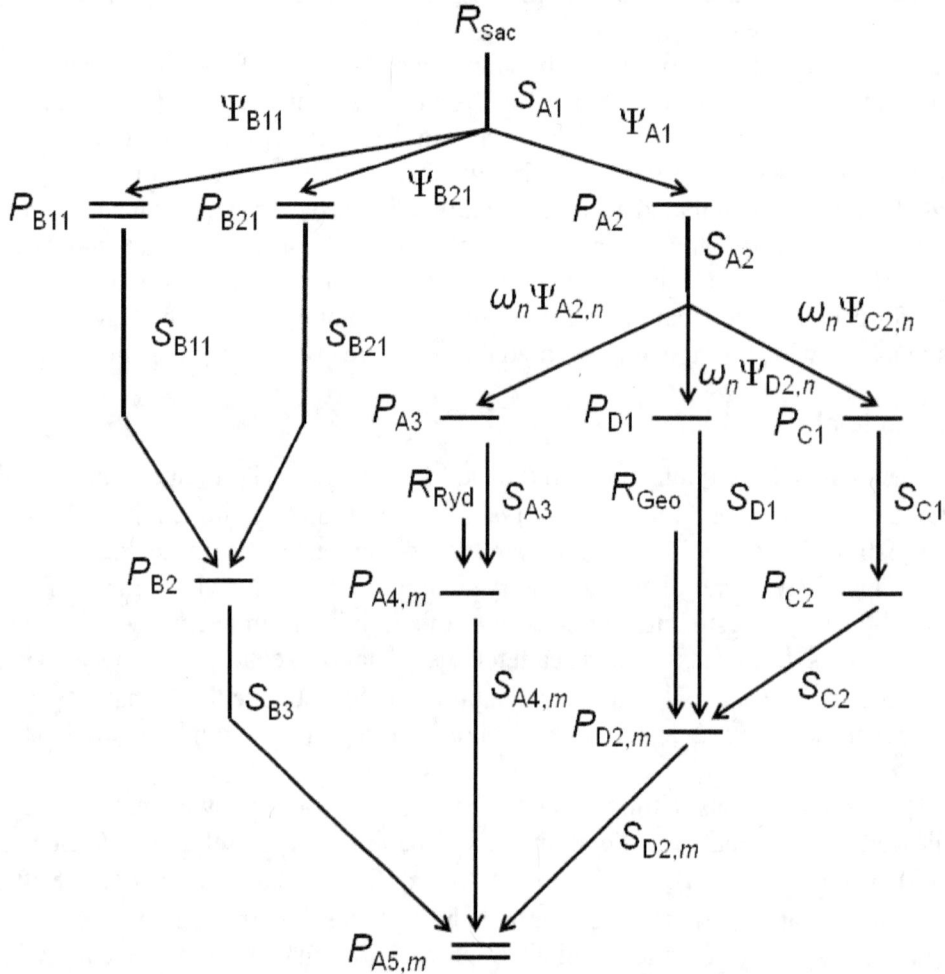

Figure 3. Schematic of the mark-recapture model used to estimate survival (S_{hi}), detection (P_{hi}), and route entrainment (Ψ_{hl}) probabilities of juvenile late fall-run Chinook salmon migrating through the Sacramento–San Joaquin River Delta, California, for releases made in winter of 2008–09. The parameter ω_n is the probability of passing the second river junction when the Delta Cross Channel was either open or closed. Release sites are denoted by R_m (m = Sac, Ryde, and Geo), parameters subscripted by n are conditional on the position of the Delta Cross Channel gate, and m denotes parameters that can be estimated separately for each release site. Locations with two parallel horizontal bars represent a dual array.

Preparation of Telemetry Data

Given the scope of the telemetry array used in this study, manual marking of data files was not feasible. Therefore, we developed an alternative automated method for processing telemetry data. When performing echo selection on data from previous studies, we relied on a combination of automated processing and manual verification that required reviewing and hand-editing each detection. This approach required an amount of staff time directly proportional to the number of acoustic tag detections contained in a dataset. For this study, we processed a representative subsample of data files to estimate the number of total detections. Based on this estimate, it was predicted that as many as 20 person years of staff time could be required to manually verify every detection in the full dataset. As a result, the CRRL and the California Water Science Center (CWSC) collaborated in the development of an automated detection algorithm that could perform echo selection on the dataset with sufficient accuracy that the manual verification of each detection would not be required. To meet this goal, echo selection was performed on a benchmark dataset and the results were evaluated for accuracy after each step in the algorithm development process and after each revision. The end result of this process was a package of software tools known as "fishCount." This package then was used to automate echo selection for the entire data-set. Based on validation tests performed using a subset of the data, the accuracy of the automated echo selection performed using fishCount was estimated as follows:

1. The echo selection is estimated to have a false positive rate of 0.3 percent (3 out of every 1,000 detections are false)
2. The echo selection is estimated to have a true detection probability of 99.5 percent (5 true detections are missed for every 1,000 detections found)

Although fishCount succeeds at extracting most true detections and eliminating most false detections, some false positives remain in the dataset, requiring application of a second level of processing. Given the probabilistic nature of the fishCount algorithm, false positives were more likely to occur at the beginning and end of detection histories for each fish. fishCount outputs detection events for each hour that a fish is detected at a telemetry node. Detection events span up to 1 h, but may be shorter if the tag is no longer detected at the telemetry node. For example, a detection history for a tag that was detected from 1:00 p.m. to 3:00 p.m. would be composed of two detection events, one spanning the 1p.m. hour and a second spanning the 2 p.m. hour. For each detection event, fishCount produces a score, with higher values reflecting a higher likelihood that a given detection event was produced by a valid transmitter. This score variable was used as part of several criteria to eliminate false positives. False positives were defined as follows: detection events occurring prior to the fish being released, detection events with a score of less than 1, detection events with a score of less than 10 and fewer than 400 pulses, detection events occurring later than 45 days after release, and detection events with a score of less than 5 and occurring 21 days after a previous detection event. These criteria were based on logical examination of the data. Tags detected prior to deployment could not be valid detections, and tags detected 45 days after deployment likely were false positives given that 100 percent of the tags in the tag-life study expired after 45 days. Score values and pulse counts of these types of detection events were evaluated to develop the aforementioned criteria. Furthermore, detection events that were impossible, owing to unrealistic fish movement rates between telemetry locations (e.g., 300 ft/s) also were examined in a similar way to derive criteria for removal of false positives.

In addition to false positives, data were analyzed for potential predation events. Predation is an inherent problem in telemetry-based juvenile salmonid survival studies, where consumed smolts are not easily distinguished from live smolts. Only one method has been proposed for addressing this issue. Vogel (2010) proposed a three-pronged approach to evaluating the state of tags (smolt or consumed smolt) moving through a telemetry array. This approach was unrealistic for this study given the large number of tags and telemetry stations. Therefore, we developed criteria for assessing and classifying tags as smolt or predator as they moved through the array based on behaviors of tagged predators reported in Vogel (2010, 2011).

Residence times and directional movement of the tag relative to direction of river flow were used to determine fish that possibly had been consumed by a predator. Each type of movement behavior was scored as 0 for smolt-like or 1 for predator-like behavior. Directional movement was one classification criterion. Dual arrays in several locations (B_{11}, B_{21}, and junction 2) allowed fine-scale determination of directional movements of tags in the system in relation to flow direction. Tags that showed continued upstream movement against the flow were flagged as potential predators (1). Additionally, fish that exceeded the 95th percentile of residence time at each telemetry station were flagged as demonstrating non-migratory or predator-like behavior. The 95th percentile of residence time was calculated from the entire population of residence times at each telemetry station owing to the consistent flows throughout the study. For each detection event, behavior that did not violate any of the aforementioned criteria was classified as 0 or smolt-like. A cumulative score for each fish then was tallied by summing the score for each behavior, with higher scores indicating a higher likelihood of predation. Fish with total behavioral scores greater than the 95th percentile of the score distribution were classified as predators. These transmitters were considered smolts up to the point at which their cumulative individual scores exceeded the 95th percentile score, after which they were identified as predators. Detection histories then were truncated at this point and used to create capture histories that were used for model parameter estimation. Survival models also were fit to non-truncated detection histories to examine the effect of predator removal on overall survival estimates. To verify this methodology, two-dimensional tracks at junction 2 were examined for predator- or smolt-like movement patterns. Junction 2 was populated with 30 nodes at the Delta Cross Channel gates, 16 at the Georgiana Slough and Sacramento River junction, and 16 at the Walnut Grove Bridge. This array of nodes allowed two-dimensional tracking of tags as they moved through the area. Movement patterns were examined for all fish moving through this area. Fish showing "looping" or "patrolling" type behaviors were classified as predator-like. After classifications were made, these determinations were compared to determinations made using the residence time and directional movement criteria.

Parameter Estimation

Detection histories describe concisely the migration and detection process of fish moving through the network of telemetry stations. For example, a fish with the history A0D0DA indicates that it was released at Sacramento ("A") and was not detected in the Sacramento River at A_2 ("0"). It subsequently was detected at the head of Georgiana Slough ("D0"), at the end of Mokelumne/Potato Slough ("D"), and at Chipps Island ("A"). Each detection history represents one cell of a multinomial distribution where the probability of each cell is defined as a function of the detection, survival, and route entrainment probabilities (see Perry and others, 2010, for an example). Given these cell probabilities, the maximum likelihood estimates are determined by maximizing the likelihood function of a multinomial distribution with respect to the parameters:

$$L_{km}\left(\underset{\sim}{\beta}\middle|R_{km},n_{jkm}\right) \propto \prod_{j=1}^{J} \pi_{jkm}^{n_{jkm}},$$ (1)

where

L_{km} is the likelihood for the kth release group ($k = 1, ..., 10$) at the mth release site (m=Sacramento (Sac), Georgiana Slough (Geo), Ryde (Ryd)),

R_{km} is the number of fish released for each release group and release site,

n_{jkm} is the number of fish with the jth detection history in the kth release group at the mth release site, and

π_{jkm} is the probability of the jth detection history in the kth release group at the mth release site expressed as a function of the parameters (β).

The likelihood was numerically maximized with respect to the parameters using algorithms provided in the software program USER (Lady and others, 2008; see appendix D). Parameters were estimated separately for each release (k) but simultaneously for all three release sites by expressing the joint likelihood as the product of $L_{k,\text{Sac}}$, $L_{k,\text{Geo}}$, and $L_{k,\text{Ryd}}$. The variance-covariance matrix was estimated as the inverse of the Hessian matrix. We used the delta method (Seber, 1982) to estimate the variance of parameters that are functions of the maximum likelihood estimates. Uncertainty in parameter estimates is presented as standard errors.

For each release, the full model was considered as the model with the fewest parameter constraints, which still allowed all parameters to be uniquely estimated. When parameter estimates occur at the boundaries of one (or zero), they cannot be estimated through iterative maximum likelihood techniques and must be set to one (or zero). In our study, many detection probabilities were set to one because all fish passing a given location were known to have been detected at that location. In some cases, survival probabilities were fixed at one because all fish detected at a given telemetry station also were detected at the next downstream location. Additionally, parameters for Route C (the Delta Cross Channel) were set to zero when the Delta Cross Channel was closed. A full detailing of parameter constraints applied under the full model is provided in appendixes A, B, and C.

The purpose of using three release areas was to reduce bias caused by potential tag failure. The Sacramento release groups likely would experience tag failure before arrival at Chipps Island; therefore, we used release groups at Ryde and Georgiana Slough to obtain unbiased survival estimates for the lower reaches of the Delta. Given tag failure rates, estimates in the lower reaches of the Delta for the Sacramento releases likely would be much lower than the estimates for fish released lower in the system at Ryde and Georgiana Slough. Our goal was to combine survival estimates from the multiple releases to minimize negative bias caused by tag failure.

Survival through the Delta

Survival through the Delta is defined as the probability of survival from the entrance to the Delta at station A_2 to the exit of the Delta at station A_5 (Chipps Island). Population-level survival through the Delta was estimated from the individual components as:

$$S_{\text{Delta}} = \sum_{h=\text{A}}^{\text{D}} \Psi_h S_h,$$ (2)

13

where

S_h is the probability of surviving the Delta given the specific migration route taken through the Delta, and

Ψ_h is the probability of migrating through the Delta using one of four migration routes (A = Sacramento River, B = Steamboat and Sutter Sloughs, C = Delta Cross Channel, D = Georgiana Slough).

Thus, population survival through the Delta is a weighted average of the route-specific survival probabilities with weights equal to the fraction of fish migrating through each route.

Migration route probabilities are a function of the route entrainment probabilities at each of the two river junctions:

$$\Psi_A = \Psi_{A1}\Psi_{A2}, \tag{3}$$

$$\Psi_B = \Psi_{B11} + \Psi_{B21}, \tag{4}$$

$$\Psi_C = \Psi_{A1}\Psi_{C2}, \text{ and} \tag{5}$$

$$\Psi_D = \Psi_{A1}\Psi_{D2}. \tag{6}$$

For instance, consider a fish that migrates through the Delta using the Delta Cross Channel (Route C). To enter the Delta Cross Channel, this fish first remains in the Sacramento River at junction 1 with probability Ψ_{A1}, after which it enters the Delta Cross Channel at the second river junction with probability Ψ_{C2}. Thus, the probability of a fish migrating through the Delta through the Delta Cross Channel (Ψ_C) is the product of these route entrainment probabilities, $\Psi_{A1}\Psi_{C2}$.

Survival through the Delta for a given migration route (S_h) is the product of the reach-specific survival probabilities that trace each migration path through the Delta between the points A_2 and A_5 (Perry and others, 2010). However, to minimize bias resulting from tag failure, we combined reach-specific survival from different release groups to estimate route-specific survival. Reach-specific survival for the Sacramento release group was used through sites A_4, B_2, and D_2 (fig. 2). The Ryde release group was used to estimate survival through the final reach of the Sacramento River (S_{A4r}), and the Georgiana Slough release group was used to estimate survival through the final reach of the interior Delta (S_{D2g}).

Survival through the Delta for fish that remain in the Sacramento River through the first and second river junctions is expressed as:

$$S_A = S_{A1}S_{A2}S_{A3}S_{A4r}. \tag{7}$$

Survival through the Delta for fish taking the Delta Cross Channel (Route C) and Georgiana Slough (Route D) is expressed similarly:

$$S_C = S_{A1}S_{A2}S_{C1}S_{C2}S_{D2g}, \text{ and} \tag{8}$$

$$S_D = S_{A1}S_{A2}S_{D1}S_{D2g}. \tag{9}$$

We combined Sutter and Steamboat Sloughs into a single migration route, but survival through the Delta can be estimated separately for fish that enter Sutter Slough and fish that enter Steamboat Slough:

$$S_B = \Psi_{B11}S_{B1} + \Psi_{B21}S_{B2}, \tag{10}$$

14

where

S_B is survival through the Delta for fish that enter either Sutter or Steamboat Sloughs,

S_B1 and $S_\text{B2}$are survival through the Delta for fish that enter Sutter and Steamboat Sloughs, respectively, and

S_B1 and $S_\text{B2}$are estimated as:

$$S_\text{B1} = S_\text{A1}S_\text{B11}S_\text{A4r} \text{, and} \tag{11}$$

$$S_\text{B2} = S_\text{A1}S_\text{B21}S_\text{A4r}. \tag{12}$$

We estimated route-specific survival and migration routing separately for each of 10 release groups, and represent season-wide estimates using a weighted mean and standard error. To estimate mean survival and routing, each release-specific parameter was weighted by CV^{-2} (CV is coefficient of variation) following methods described by Burnham and others (1987).

Results

Tag Life

From October 28, 2008, through December 8, 2008, water temperature in the holding tank matched the 10-year daily mean water temperatures (1999–2008) in the Sacramento River at the RIV gaging station. Starting on December 9, 2008, tank temperature was matched to the daily mean at Rio Vista. Temperature in the tank started at 13.6°C, and was 10.9°C when the study ended. It should be noted that temperatures decreased suddenly on three occasions: a boiler malfunction caused temperatures to decrease to 6.3°C for 61 hours, a power outage caused temperatures to decrease to 8°C for 4 hours, and a pump malfunction caused temperatures to decrease to 3.1°C for 79 hours. Such decreases in temperature are expected to reduce actual tag life, thereby making our estimates more conservative than would normally be expected in the Sacramento River during this time of year.

The average life of the 795-E tags was 22.4 d (figs. 4, 5, and 6). Three tags expired after 12 d and the last tag expired after 45.3 d. For fish released at the Sacramento site, approximately 90–98 percent of detected tags were still operational upon fish arrival at downstream locations (figs. 4 and 5). For fish released at the two lower locations, only 85–90 percent of the tags were operational upon arriving at downstream telemetry stations (figs. 5 and 6). This suggests that our survival estimates represent the joint probability of tag survival and fish survival rather than fish survival only. As such, survival estimates presented are negatively biased.

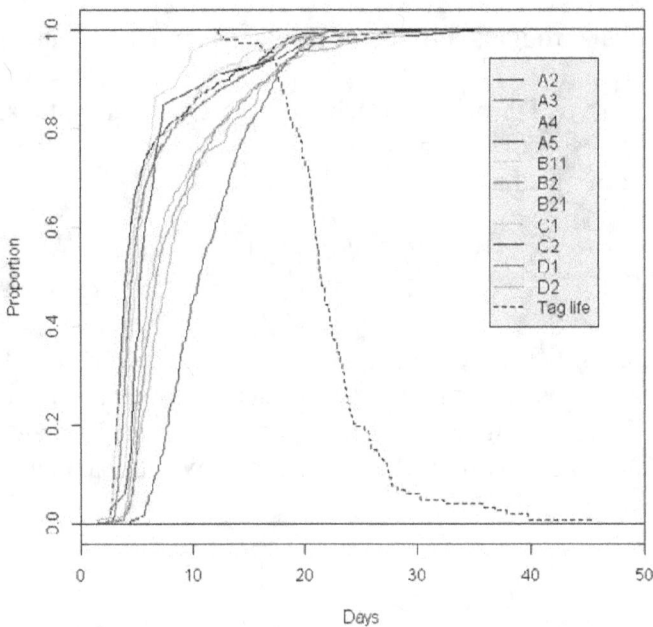

Figure 4. Tag life and travel time of fish released at Sacramento, California, and arriving at downstream stations. The dashed line represents tag-life survival distribution function. Other lines represent the cumulative distribution of arrival time to each telemetry station.

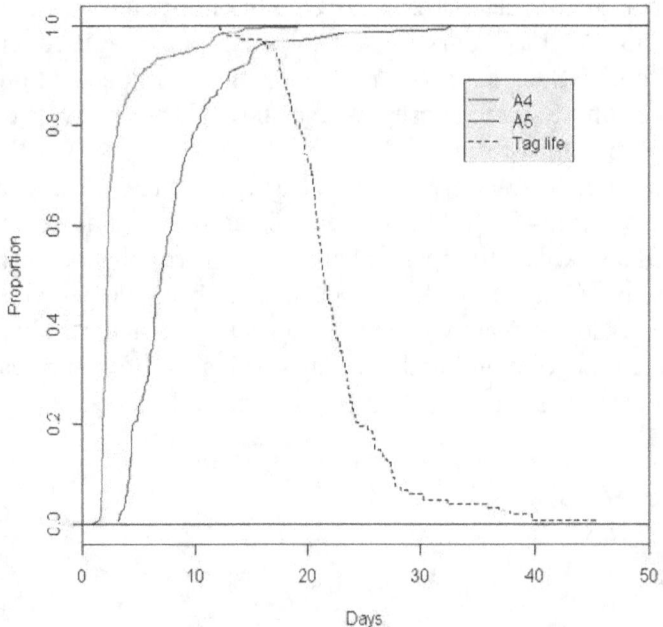

Figure 5. Tag life and travel times for fish released at the Ryde release site, Sacramento-San Joaquin River Delta, California, and arriving at downstream stations. The dashed line represents tag-life survival distribution function. Other lines represent the cumulative distribution of arrival time to each telemetry station.

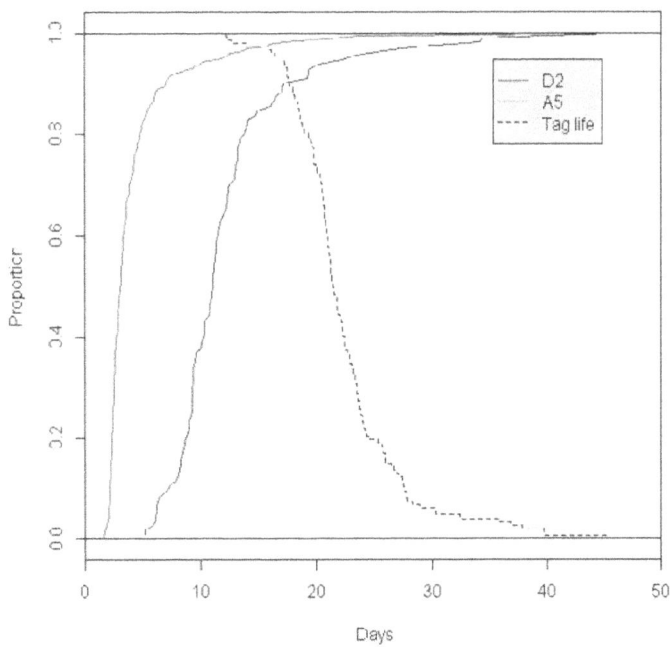

Figure 6. Tag life and travel times for fish released at Georgiana Slough release site, Sacramento-San Joaquin River Delta, California, and arriving at downstream stations. The dashed line represents tag-life survival distribution function. Other lines represent the cumulative distribution of arrival time to each telemetry station.

River Conditions and Migration Timing

River conditions remained fairly constant throughout the study period. Discharge in the Sacramento River at Freeport was approximately 10,000 ft^3/s during all releases (fig. 7). A spike in flow occurred at the end of December 2008 and the end of January 2009 (fig. 7). Median travel times for fish released at the Sacramento release site to the second junction (Stations A_3, C_1, and D_1 in fig. 2) were fairly consistent throughout the study (range=2.78 d for R_7, and 5.29 d for R_4). Releases 4, 5, and 8 had the greatest variability in travel times, with some fish taking more than 15 d to reach the junction. Fish from R_7 took the shortest amount of time to reach the junction, with 75 percent of the fish arriving at the junction in approximately 4 d. The increase in discharge to about 15,000 ft^3/s just prior to the release of these fish may have contributed to their faster travel times (fig. 7). Fish from R_4 took the longest amount of time to reach the junction. After 12 d, only 75 percent of the fish had reached the junction. Release 4 was associated with the lowest flows during the study period.

For fish released at Ryde and Georgiana Slough, median travel time to Chipps Island ranged from 3.16 d for R_1 to 8.91 d for R_9 (fig. 8). All other groups had median travel times of 7–8 d to Chipps Island. Between-group travel times for the downstream release groups were less variable than for the Sacramento releases. In general, 90 percent of the fish released at the downstream locations arrived at Chipps Island about 12–14 d after release (fig. 8).

17

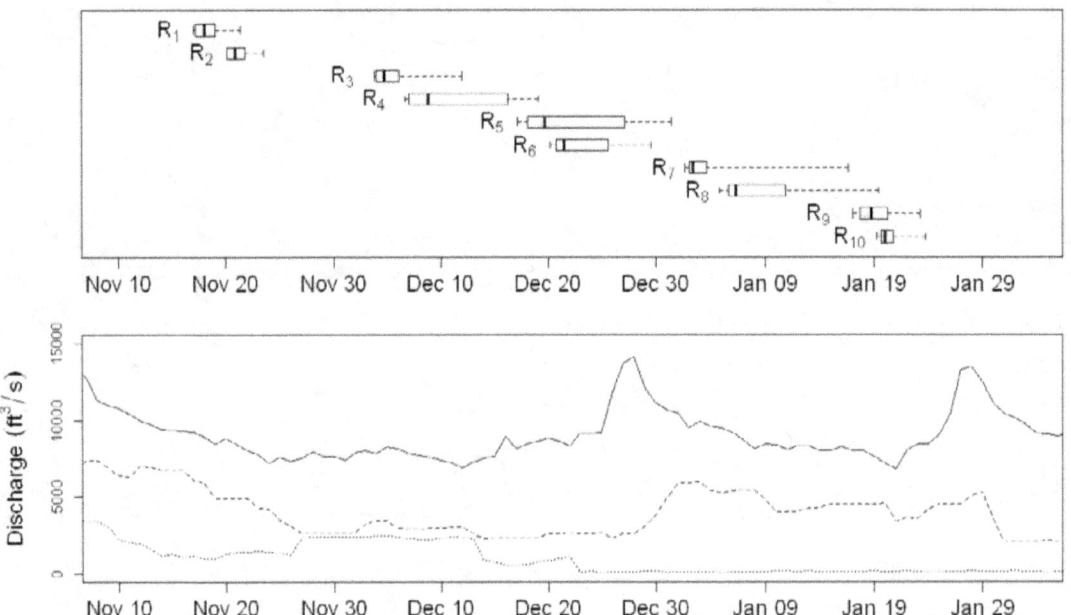

Figure 7. Graphs showing river discharge, water exports, and Delta Cross Channel discharge during the migration period of tagged juvenile Chinook salmon migrating through the Sacramento-San Joaquin River Delta, California, during winter of 2008–09. Boxplots show the distribution of arrival dates at Junction 2 on the Sacramento River by fish released at Sacramento. The symbols R_1-R_{10} are plotted at the release dates. Whiskers represent the 10th and 90th percentiles, the box encompasses the 25th to 75th percentiles, and the line bisecting the box is the median arrival date. River discharge (solid line) is average daily discharge of the Sacramento River at Freeport (near telemetry station A_2), Delta Cross Channel discharge (dotted line) is the daily average discharge, and water exports (dashed line) are the total daily discharge of water exported from the Delta at the pumping projects.

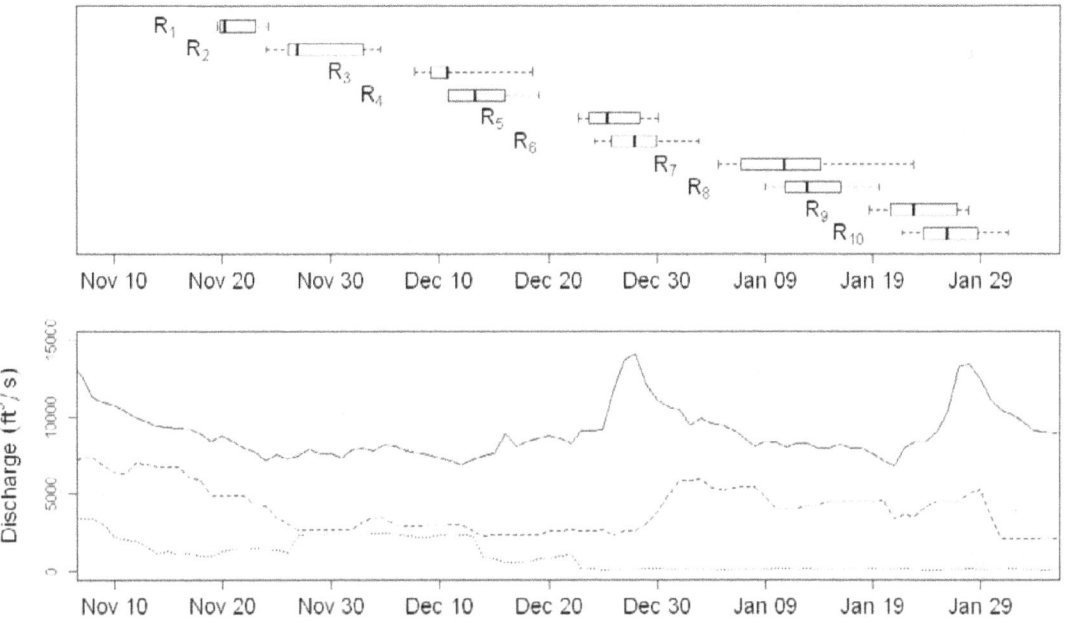

Figure 8. Graphs showing river discharge, water exports, and Delta Cross Channel discharge during the migration period of tagged juvenile Chinook salmon migrating through the Sacramento-San Joaquin River Delta, California, during winter of 2008–09. Boxplots show the distribution of arrival dates at Chipps Island (A_5) of fish released at Ryde and Georgiana Slough. The symbols R_1-R_{10} are plotted at the release dates. Whiskers represent the 10th and 90th percentiles, the box encompasses the 25th to 75th percentiles, and the line bisecting the box is the median arrival date. River discharge (solid line) is average daily discharge of the Sacramento River at Freeport (near telemetry station A_2), Delta Cross Channel discharge (dotted line) is the daily average discharge, and water exports (dashed line) are the total daily discharge of water exported from the Delta at the pumping projects.

Detection Probabilities

For all release groups, detection probabilities at many telemetry stations were high (see appendix A; table A1). Detection probabilities ranged from 0.5 ($P_{D2,Sac}$, R_1) to 1.00 for many locations and release groups throughout the study. For each location, detection probabilities remained fairly constant for all release groups. Overall, detection probabilities for the first two release groups were the lowest. The dual arrays (P_{B11}, P_{B21}, P_{A5}) had detection probabilities greater than 0.90 with the exception of $P_{A5, Ryd}$ and $P_{A5,Sac}$ for R_1 and $P_{A5,Geo}$ for R_2.

Route-Specific Survival through the Delta

Due to evidence of premature tag failure, route-specific and total survival through the Delta were calculated using survival estimates of fish released at Sacramento to A_4 and D_2 and estimates of survival for Ryde and Georgiana Slough release groups to Chipps Island (fig. 3). Total survival through the Delta (S_{Delta}) ranged from 0.019 for R_2 to 0.277 for R_6 (table 2). The overall weighted mean for S_{Delta} was 0.188 (standard error of 0.023). Survival was lowest for the four groups released from November 14, 2008, to December 6, 2008. These releases occurred during decreasing flows in the Delta. Release 6 had the highest estimated survival

(S_{Delta} = 0.277). This release occurred during one of the peak discharge events between December 14 and 20, 2008. However, travel times by other release groups were shorter. Travel time for all other releases did not appear to have a direct affect on survival. Release 7 had the shortest travel times, but survival for this release group was only 0.108 (table 2) and only slightly above the median overall survival estimate.

Route-specific survival was variable between release groups. Fish remaining in the Sacramento River (Route A) had the highest survival for 6 of the 10 releases (table 2; figs. 9 and 10). Fish migrating through the interior Delta (Routes C and D) has the lowest survival for all releases with the exception of R_2 (Route C, fig. 9). This estimate was driven by a single fish that migrated through Route C for this release. Fish migrating through Route B had the highest survival for releases R_8, R_9, and R_{10} (fig. 10) followed by Route A.

Survival patterns within Route B (Sutter and Steamboat Sloughs) were consistent between release groups. Survival generally was higher for Steamboat Slough (S_{B2}) than for Sutter Slough (S_{B1}; table 2; fig. 11), with the exception of R_8. Survival for Steamboat Slough was similar to survival estimates for Sacramento River for all release groups.

Percentages of fish migrating through the interior Delta influenced the overall survival through the Delta. Overall survival decreased as percentages of fish entering the interior Delta increased because survival through the interior Delta was consistently lower than for other migration routes (figs. 9 and 10).

Table 2. Route-specific survival through the Sacramento–San Joaquin River Delta (S_h; h= Route A, B, C, or D), California, and the probability of migrating through each route (Ψ_h; h= Route A, B, C, or D) for acoustically tagged fall-run juvenile Chinook salmon from 10 release groups during winter 2008–09.

[Population survival through the Delta (S_{Delta}) is the average of route-specific survival weighted by the probability of migrating through each route. Values in parentheses represent standard error. Overall mean is the weighted average of release-specific estimates, with weights equal to the inverse relative variance squared. The Delta Cross Channel gates were closed for releases 8, 9, and 10. Mean values of the routing probabilities are not constrained to sum to 1]

Release	S_A	S_B	S_C	S_D	Ψ_A	Ψ_B	Ψ_C	Ψ_D	S_{Delta}
1	0.135(0.039)	0.051(0.035)	0.000(NA)	0.058(0.048)	0.560(0.055)	0.106(0.030)	0.046(0.022)	0.288(0.050)	0.098(0.027)
2	0.012(0.012)	0.008(0.009)	0.119(0.088)	0.052(0.041)	0.495(0.051)	0.322(0.046)	0.011(0.011)	0.172(0.039)	0.019(0.012)
3	0.038(0.019)	0.025(0.014)	0.019(0.019)	0.004(0.004)	0.333(0.055)	0.349(0.049)	0.275(0.052)	0.043(0.024)	0.027(0.012)
4	0.119(0.036)	0.100(0.033)	0.071(0.038)	0.066(0.029)	0.457(0.054)	0.263(0.043)	0.072(0.028)	0.208(0.046)	0.100(0.025)
5	0.262(0.048)	0.208(0.043)	0.120(0.091)	0.195(0.056)	0.511(0.041)	0.288(0.036)	0.014(0.010)	0.187(0.032)	0.232(0.037)
6	0.306(0.050)	0.290(0.053)	0.162(0.074)	0.179(0.042)	0.500(0.043)	0.318(0.039)	0.023(0.013)	0.159(0.032)	0.277(0.041)
7	0.126(0.031)	0.087(0.026)	0.000(NA)	0.088(0.026)	0.547(0.046)	0.228(0.037)	0.009(0.009)	0.215(0.039)	0.108(0.023)
8	0.233(0.040)	0.259(0.047)	NA	0.121(0.033)	0.539(0.046)	0.305(0.040)	NA	0.155(0.034)	0.223(0.035)
9	0.199(0.036)	0.236(0.046)	NA	0.094(0.029)	0.507(0.048)	0.259(0.040)	NA	0.234(0.041)	0.184(0.029)
10	0.099(0.029)	0.120(0.036)	NA	0.093(0.033)	0.516(0.050)	0.265(0.041)	NA	0.219(0.043)	0.103(0.024)
Overall mean	0.211(0.025)	0.210(0.025)	0.099(0.024)	0.127(0.016)	0.512(0.014)	0.288(0.270)	0.184(0.064)	0.207(0.188)	0.188(0.023)

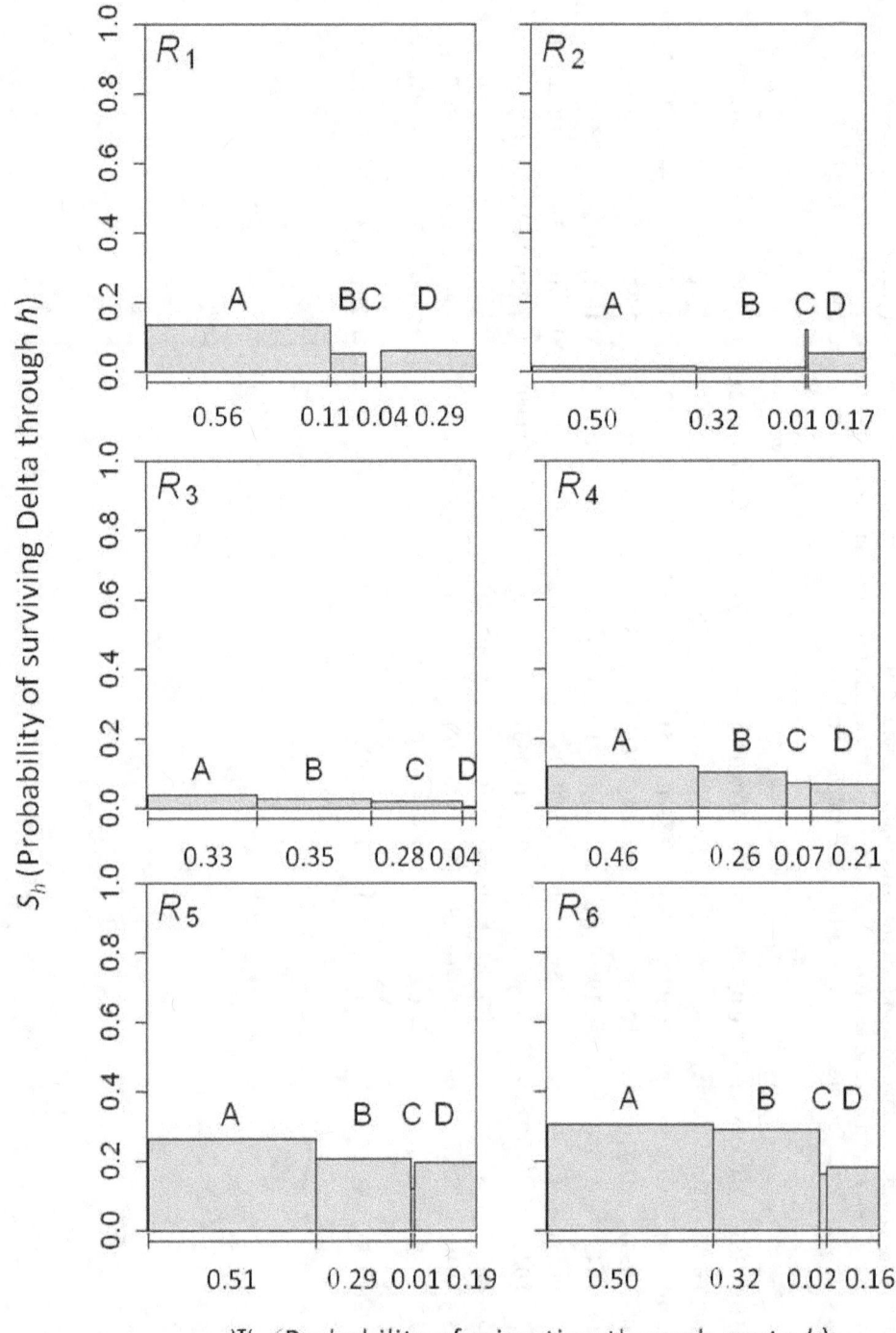

Figure 9. Graphs showing probability of surviving migration through the Sacramento-San Joaquin River Delta (S_h), California, for each of four migration routes for tagged late-fall juvenile Chinook salmon migrating from the Sacramento River. The width of each bar shows the fraction of fish migrating through each route (Ψ_h), and the total area under the bars yields S_{Delta}. Labels A–D represent the Sacramento River, Steamboat and Sutter Sloughs, the Delta Cross Channel, and Georgiana Slough, respectively. Panels are labeled by release groups ($R_1 - R_6$).

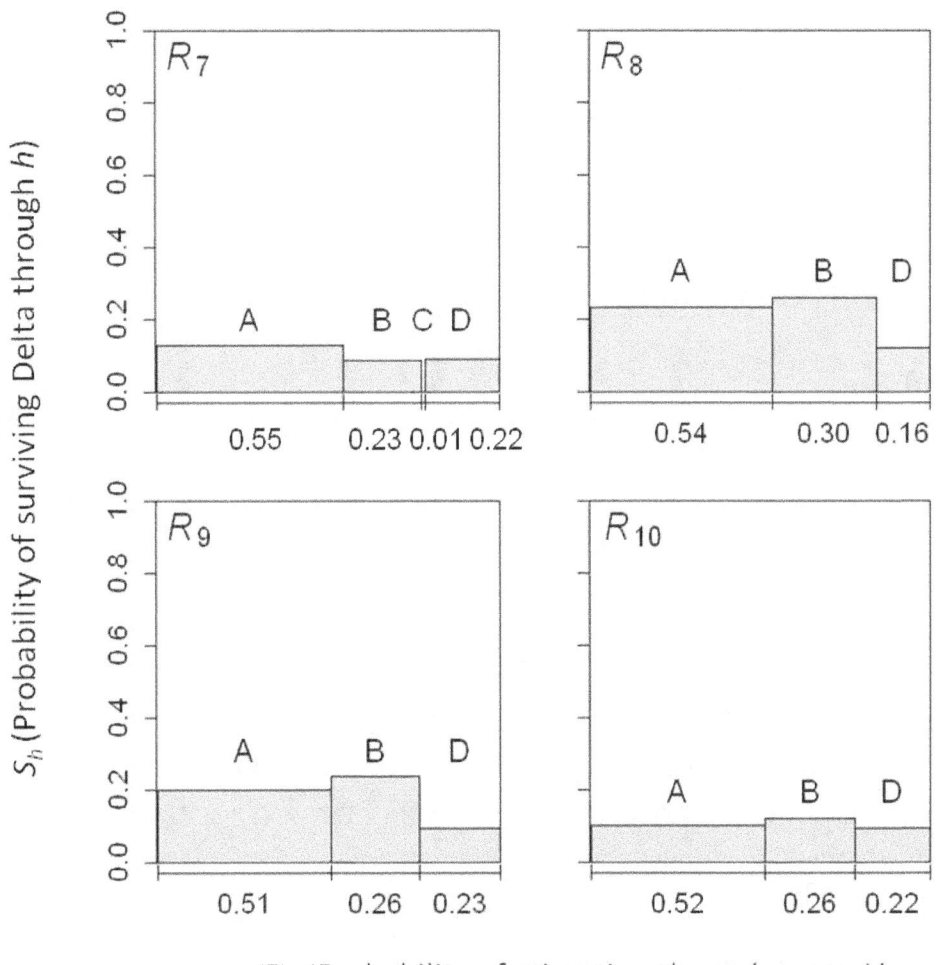

Figure 10. Graph showing probability of surviving migration through the Sacramento-San Joaquin River Delta (S_h), California, for each of four migration routes for tagged late-fall juvenile Chinook salmon migrating from the Sacramento River. The width of each bar shows the fraction of fish migrating through each route (Ψ_h), and the total area under the bars yields S_{Delta}. Labels A–D represent the Sacramento River, Steamboat and Sutter Sloughs, the Delta Cross Channel, and Georgiana Slough, respectively. Panels are labeled by release groups ($R_7 – R_{10}$). The Delta Cross Channel gates were closed for all fish encountering the junction in releases R_8, R_9, and R_{10}.

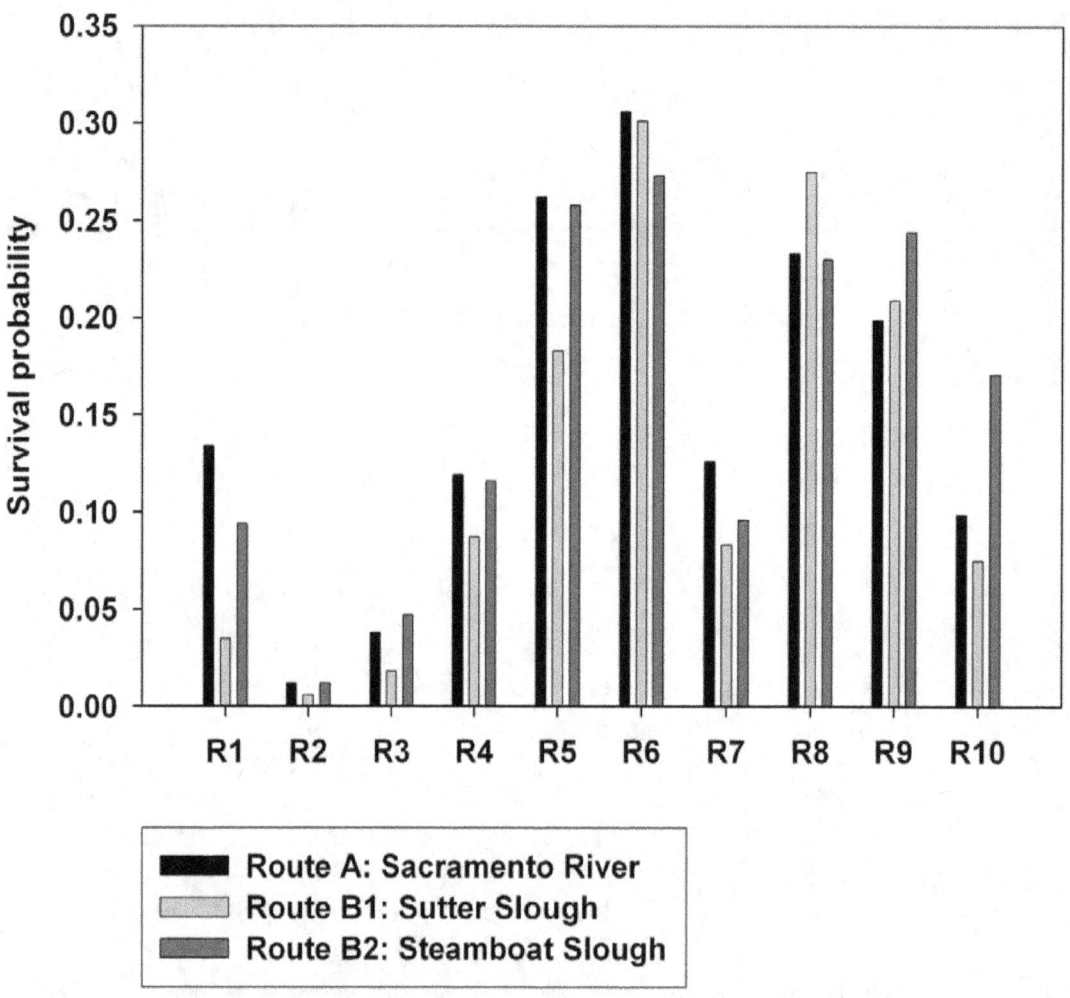

Figure 11. Graph showing comparison of route-specific survival between the Sacramento River (A), Sutter Slough (B_1), and Steamboat Slough (B_2), California, for late fall-run Chinook salmon tagged and released in winter 2008–09.

Migration Routing

Migration routing at the first junction, (Sutter Slough, Steamboat Slough, and Sacramento River) was consistent between release groups (appendix B, table B1). Estimates of Ψ_{A1} ranged from 0.651 to 0.894, indicating that most fish remained in the Sacramento River. Of the fish entering Sutter and Steamboat Sloughs, most migrated through Sutter Slough, Route B1 (appendix B, table B1).

Migration routing at the second junction depended on the status of the Delta Cross Channel gates when fish migrated through the junction. The gates were open only for releases 1–7 (table 3). These release groups entered the junction when the gates were both open and closed during the migration period of each release group. The probability of fish encountering the gates when they were open (ω_{open}) ranged from 0.012 (R_7) to 0.911 (R_3). Of the fish that entered the junction when the gates were open, entrainment into the Delta Cross Channel ranged from 13.6 to 66.7 percent (with the exception of R_7, for which entrainment was 100 percent owing to a single fish passing the junction when the gate was open; appendix B, table B1). On average, 47 percent of the fish that entered the junction when the gates were open were entrained into the Delta Cross Channel.

Migration route probabilities account for the joint probability of route entrainment at both river junctions and indicate the fraction of the population using each migration route. We observed that with the cross channel gate closed, the fraction of fish remaining in the Sacramento River was higher ($\Psi_{A,Closed}$) for all release groups than when the gate was open ($\Psi_{A,open}$; table 3). Additionally, migration route probabilities for Georgiana Slough (Ψ_D) were higher with the gates closed than with the gates open. These results indicate that operation of the Delta Cross Channel entrains fish that otherwise would have remained in the Sacramento River or entered Georgiana Slough. For fish passing the Delta Cross Channel when it was open, the overall probability of migrating to the interior Delta through the Delta Cross Channel ranged from 0.00 to 0.186 (table 3).

Aggregating over open and closed gate operations for each release group, the Sacramento River was the primary migration route taken by all releases except for R_3, with 33–56 percent of fish migrating through this route (Route A; table 2). Sutter and Steamboat Sloughs (Route B) ranked second for all releases except for R_1, where a higher proportion of fish entered Georgiana Slough (table 2; fig. 9), and R_3, where the greatest percentage of fish migrated through Route B. Because most release groups experienced both open and closed gate conditions, a relatively small fraction of fish entered the Delta Cross Channel (Route C). For all but one release, less than 10 percent of each release group entered the Delta Cross Channel. Entrainment into Georgiana Slough (Route D) ranged from 4.3 to 28.8 percent among release groups (table 2).

Table 3. Probability of migrating through each route (Ψ_h; h=Route A, B, C, or D) for acoustically tagged late fall-run juvenile Chinook salmon released in winter 2008–09 conditional on gate position when fish entered junction 2, Sacramento-San Joaquin River Delta, California.

[Values in parentheses represent standard error. Migration routing probabilities for Route B are the same for both gate positions]

Release	$\Psi_{A,Open}$	$\Psi_{B,Open/closed}$	$\Psi_{C,Open}$	$\Psi_{D,Open}$	$\Psi_{A,Closed}$	$\Psi_{D,Closed}$	ω_{open}
1	0.298(0.172)	0.106(0.030)	0.596(0.173)	0(0)	0.582(0.056)	0.312(0.054)	0.077(0.030)
2	0.339(0.171)	0 322(0.046)	0.170(0.147)	0.170(0.147)	0.506(0.051)	0.172(0.04)	0.063(0.031)
3	0.317(0.056)	0 349(0.049)	0.302(0.056)	0.032(0.022)	0.488(0.146)	0.163(0.141)	0.911(0.042)
4	0.451(0.062)	0 263(0.043)	0.100(0.039)	0.186(0.052)	0.473(0.095)	0.265(0.092)	0.720(0.060)
5	0.285(0.157)	0 288(0.036)	0.280(0.156)	0.147(0.130)	0.522(0.042)	0.189(0.033)	0.049(0.021)
6	0.426(0.119)	0 318(0.039)	0.256(0.118)	0(0)	0.507(0.044)	0.175(0.034)	0.089(0.030)
7	0(0)	0 228(0.037)	0.772(0.037)	0(0)	0.554(0.046)	0.218(0.039)	0.012(0.012)
8	NA	0 305(0.040)	NA	NA	0.539(0.046)	0.155(0.034)	NA
9	NA	0 259(0.040)	NA	NA	0.507(0.048)	0.234(0.041)	NA
10	NA	0 265(0.041)	NA	NA	0.516(0.050)	0.219(0.043)	NA

Predation Events

Our analyses classified 117 fish as showing predator like-behavior. The break point for smolt-like or predator-like behavior (i.e, the 95th percentile) was a total behavioral score of 66 predator-like behaviors (fig. 12). The detection histories for these fish were truncated at the detection event at which the cumulative behavioral score was greater than 66. Examination of 2D tracks of tags passing through the Delta Cross Channel and the Georgiana Slough junction supported the classifications assigned by our approach. Overall, removal of predators had little effect on the estimate of S_{Delta}. At most, the removal of predators decreased survival estimates by 2 percentage points (table 4). This suggests our survival estimates at the scale of an entire migration route are robust to consumption of tagged smolts by predators. However, using a predator-detection algorithm to classify fish as predator-like is critical because reach-specific survival estimates are more likely to be biased by predators moving among reaches within the study area.

Figure 12. Histogram showing cumulative behavioral scores for the predator filter algorithm. The red vertical line (Cumulative Score = 66) represents the 95th percentile. The x and y axes are truncated for clarity.

Table 4. Comparison of total survival estimates for truncated capture histories and non-truncated capture histories of Chinook salmon, Sacramento-San Joaquin River Delta, California.

[Values in parentheses represent the standard error. Overall mean is the weighted mean]

Release	S_{Delta} predators removed	S_{Delta} predators not removed
1	0.098 (0.027)	0.104 (0.029)
2	0.019 (0.012)	0.021 (0.013)
3	0.027 (0.012)	0.034 (0.016)
4	0.100 (0.025)	0.109 (0.027)
5	0.232 (0.037)	0.244 (0.039)
6	0.277 (0.041)	0.277 (0.041)
7	0.108 (0.023)	0.112 (0.024)
8	0.223 (0.035)	0.236 (0.036)
9	0.184 (0.029)	0.208 (0.031)
10	0.103 (0.024)	0.121 (0.028)
Mean	0.188 (0.023)	0.199 (0.023)

Discussion

Because of slow travel times coupled with short tag life, survival estimates from this study were low when compared to previous survival estimates of juvenile Chinook salmon in the Delta. As such, these estimates are negatively biased by tag failure. Caution should be exercised when interpreting these estimates on an absolute basis because they represent the probability of both the fish surviving and the tag remaining operational. In contrast, differences in survival among routes were similar to previous years, with the Sacramento River representing a high-survival route relative to the interior Delta. Therefore, while the absolute magnitude of survival is negatively biased, relative comparisons of survival between routes appear to remain robust to tag failure. Furthermore, migration routing parameters (Ψ) should remain unbiased in the presence of tag failure.

Three lines of evidence indicate that tag failure was the primary cause of low survival estimates observed in this study. First, the tag-life study showed that tags began failing after only 12 d, which is much less than travel times typically observed through the Delta (Perry and others, 2010). Second, our estimates were 25–50 percent lower than previous survival estimates in the Delta (Perry and others 2010, 2012a), which is consistent with the negative bias that would be expected, given the evidence of tag failure. For example, Perry and others (2012a) estimated S_{Delta} ranging from 0.174 to 0.543 for the winters of 2006–07 to 2008–09. Third, for four of the release groups (R_3, R_4, R_9, and R_{10}), survival estimates were much lower than for tagged fish released in conjunction with a study conducted by the U.S. Fish and Wildlife Service (USFWS; Perry and Skalski, 2010). The fish in the USFWS study were tagged and released simultaneously with fish from this study. S_{Delta} for R_3 and R_4 were 0.027 and 0.100, respectively, whereas S_{Delta} for USFWS fish released simultaneously with R_3 and R_4 was 0.386. Likewise, S_{Delta} for R_9 and R_{10} was 0.103 and 0.188, whereas survival of tagged fish from the USFWS study was 0.339 for fish released simultaneously with R_9 and R_{10}. The USFWS study used acoustic transmitters with a 70-d expected battery life; therefore, the survival estimates likely were unaffected by tag failure. These findings provide strong evidence of negative bias induced by tag failure.

In designing our study, we took steps to guard against modest tag failure, but higher-than-expected tag failure combined with low flows and consequent long travel times offset these efforts to eliminate bias. The primary purpose of releasing fish at two sites further downstream in the Delta was to obtain survival estimates through the lower Delta that were unaffected by tag failure. We tagged fish at the release sites rather than at the hatchery because tagging fish at the hatchery would have used considerable battery life prior to release of fish. Despite these efforts, the cumulative travel time distributions for fish released from lower Delta sites revealed that transmitters began failing before all fish passed Chipps Island (figs. 5 and 6). Although our approach of combining survival estimates from different release sites reduced bias resulting from tag failure, it could not eliminate the bias.

Inferences about migration routing remain unbiased in the presence of tag failure. As with other studies, the Sacramento River was the primary migration route used by tagged fish (Perry and others, 2010, 2012b). Sutter and Steamboat Sloughs had the second highest routing probability for most releases. Routing probabilities for Sutter and Steamboat Sloughs were higher than for the Sacramento River for the January releases. Perry and others (2012a) showed similar results.

Migration through the interior Delta was low for all releases. At most, the probability of being entrained into the interior Delta was 0.32 (R_3). For this release group, a large fraction of fish encountered the Delta Cross Channel when the gates were open ($\omega_{open} = 0.91$) and were subsequently entrained into the Delta Cross Channel. The probability of migrating through Route C for this release was 0.28, whereas all other estimates for entrainment into the Delta Cross Channel were less than 0.08. The maximum entrainment probability observed by Perry and others (2012a) during migration years 2006–07 to 2008–09 for Route C was 0.23 (December 2006). Aside from release 3, entrainment into the interior Delta occurred from Georgiana Slough. Entrainment into the interior Delta from Georgiana Slough ranged from 0.04 to 0.28, and was highest when flows were at their maximum during the study (R_1).

Relative survival between migration routes was consistent with previously published works. Fish migrating through the Sacramento River had the highest probability of survival for most releases, relative to alternative routes. Survival estimates for Sutter and Steamboat Sloughs were higher than those for the Sacramento River for the January 2009 releases (R_8, R_9, R_{10}). This is consistent with results presented by Perry and others (2012a). For one release group (R_2), survival for the interior Delta was more than 10 percentage points greater than survival in other routes (fig. 9). Furthermore, survival for all routes was extremely low for R_2. For example, the survival rate for the Sacramento River was only 0.012, an order of magnitude less than the mean survival rate (0.211, table 2). Additionally, survival for Sutter and Steamboat Sloughs was less than 1 percent for this release group. For all other releases, survival was lowest for fish entering the interior Delta through the Delta Cross Channel.

Our predator determination methods classified approximately five percent of detected tags as exhibiting predator-like behavior within the acoustic array at some point in their migration. This agrees closely with previously published values. Perry and others (2012b) estimated observed predation rates of 6 percent during the 2009–10 migration year, and values typically range from 6 to 10 percent. Our method only allows for determination of tags that are detected within the array and does not account for other sources of mortality such as avian predators, entrainment into water export facilities, handling stress, or poor environmental conditions. Additionally, for a tag to be classified, it must have been detected within the array. A tag that was released and not detected may or may not have been consumed by a predator. Without detections of the tag, we could not classify the source of mortality. Furthermore, survival estimates from multi-state mark recapture approaches are estimates of the joint probability of tag and fish survival. The approach we used allows for adjustment in the break-point at which tags were classified as smolts or predators and is easily modified to meet the criteria of the user. The approach is based on objective criteria rather subjective determinations and allows for multiple survival estimates to be generated from different break-point values without excessive re-examination of the data. With 5 percent of detected fish classified as predators, survival estimates decreased approximately 1–2 percentage points.

Given the results of this study, methodologies must be developed that address bias induced by tag failure. Statistical methods exist to correct survival estimates for tag failure (Cowen and Schwarz, 2005; Townsend and others, 2006), but our research indicates that these methods fail to completely remove the bias. These methods use the observed travel-time distribution to estimate the average probability of tag failure, which is then used to back-calculate true fish survival. However, in the presence of tag failure, the travel-time distribution also is negatively biased because fish with long travel times are not detected. Therefore, the estimate of the average probability of tag failure also is negatively biased, and the procedure will remove some but not all of the bias from the survival estimate (Holbrook and others, 2013).

Acknowledgments

Our analysis would not have been possible without the extensive efforts of U.S. Geological Survey field staff and collaboration with staff of the U.S. Fish and Wildlife Service, the Coleman National Fish Hatchery, and the California Department of Water Resources.

References

Baker, P.F., and Morhardt, J.E., 2001, Survival of Chinook salmon smolts in the Sacramento-San Joaquin Delta and Pacific Ocean, *in* Brown, R.L., ed., Contributions to the biology of Central Valley salmonids: Sacramento, California, California Department of Fish and Game, Fish Bulletin, 179, v. 2, p. 163–182.

Brandes, P.L., and McLain, J.S., 2001, Juvenile Chinook salmon abundance, distribution, and survival in the Sacramento-San Joaquin Estuary, *in* Brown, R.L., ed., Contributions to the biology of Central Valley salmonids: Sacramento, California, California Department of Fish and Game, Fish Bulletin 179, v.2, p. 39 –138.

Burnham, K.P., Anderson, D.R., White, G.C., Brownie, C., and Pollock, K.H., 1987, Design and analysis methods for fish survival experiments based on release-recapture: Bethesda, Maryland, American Fisheries Society, Monograph 5, 437 p.

Calfed Bay-Delta Program, 2012, Calfed science program workshops—Independent review of the regional salmon outmigration study plan workshop: Calfed Bay-Delta Program Archived Website, accessed December 21, 2012, at: *http://www.science.calwater.ca.gov/events/workshops/workshop_outmigration.html.*

California Department of Water Resources, 2013, California Data Exchange Center—Historical Data Selector: Website, accessed June 13, 2013, at http://cdec.water.ca.gov/selectQuery.html.

Cowen, L., and Schwarz, C.J., 2005, Capture-recapture studies using radio telemetry with premature radio-tag failure: Biometrics, v. 61, p. 657–664.

Holbrook, C.M., Perry, R.W., Brandes, P.L., and Adams, N.S., 2013, Adjusting survival estimates for premature transmitter failure—A case study from the Sacramento-San Joaquin Delta: Environmental Biology of Fishes, v. 96, p. 165–173.

Kimmerer, W.J. 2008. Losses of Sacramento River Chinook salmon and delta smelt (*Hypomesus transpacificus*) to entrainment in water diversions in the Sacramento-San Joaquin Delta. San Francisco Estuary and Watershed Science, v. 6 (2).

Kjelson, M.A., Raquel, P.F., and Fisher, F.W, 1981, Influences of freshwater inflow on Chinook salmon (*Oncorhynchus tshawytscha*) in the Sacramento-San Joaquin Estuary, *in* Cross, R.D., and Williams, D.L., eds., Proceedings of the National Symposium on Freshwater Inflow to Estuaries: U.S. Fish and Wildlife Service, FWS/OBS-81/04, v. 2, p. 88–108.

Lady, J.M., Westhagen, P., and Skalski, J.R., 2008, USER 4—User specified estimation routine: Seattle, University of Washington, School of Aquatic and Fishery Sciences, software application, accessed August, 2011, at *http://www.cbr.washington.edu/paramest/user/.*

Myers, J.M., Kope, R.G., Bryant, G.J., Teel, D., Lierheimer, L.J., Wainwright, T.C., Grant, W.S., Waknitz, F.W., Neely, K., Lindley, S.T., and Waples, R.S., 1998, Status review of Chinook salmon from Washington, Idaho, Oregon, and California: National Oceanic and Atmospheric Administration Technical Memorandum, NFMS-NWFSC-35.

Newman, K.B., 2003, Modelling paired release-recovery data in the presence of survival and capture heterogeneity with application to marked juvenile salmon: Statistical Modelling, v. 3, p. 157–177.

Newman, K.B, 2008, An evaluation of four Sacramento-San Joaquin River Delta juvenile salmon survival studies: U.S. Fish and Wildlife Service, Stockton, California, Project number SCI-06-G06-299, accessed August, 2008.

Newman, K.B., and Brandes, P.L., 2010, Hierarchical modeling of juvenile Chinook salmon survival as a function of Sacramento-San Joaquin Delta water exports: North American Journal of Fisheries Management, v. 30, p. 157–169.

Newman, K.B., and Rice, J., 2002, Modeling the survival of Chinook salmon smolts outmigrating through the lower Sacramento River system: Journal of the American Statistical Association, v. 97, p. 983–993.

National Marine Fisheries Service, 1997, NMFS proposed recovery plan for the Sacramento River winter-run Chinook: National Marine Fisheries Service, Southwest Regional Office, Long Beach, California.

National Oceanic and Atmospheric Administration, 2008, Fisheries off West Coast states and in the western Pacific, West Coast salmon fisheries, 2008 management measures and a temporary rule: Federal Register, v. 73, p. 23971–23981.

Nehlsen, W., Williams, J.E., and Lichatowich, J. A., 1991, Pacific salmon at the crossroads—Stocks at risk from California, Oregon, Idaho, and Washington: Fisheries, v. 16, p. 4–21.

Nichols, F.H., Cloern, J.E., Luoma, S.N., and Peterson, D.H., 1986, The modification of an estuary: Science, v. 4738, p. 567–573.

Perry, R.W., Brandes, P., Burau, J., Klimley, A., MacFarlane, B., Michel, C., and Skalski, J., 2012a, Sensitivity of survival to migration routes used by juvenile Chinook salmon to negotiate the Sacramento-San Joaquin River Delta: Environmental Biology of Fishes, p. 1–12, doi:10.1007/s10641-012-9984-6.

Perry, R.W., Romine, J.G., Brewer, S.J., LaCivita, P.E., Brostoff, W.N., and Chapman, E.D. 2012b, Survival and migration route probabilities of juvenile Chinook salmon in the Sacramento-San Joaquin River Delta during the winter of 2009–10: U.S. Geological Survey Open-File Report 2012-1200, 30 p.

Perry, R.W., and Skalski, J.R., 2010, Individual-, release-, and route-specific variation in survival of juvenile Chinook salmon migrating through the Sacramento-San Joaquin River Delta: Stockton, California, Report to U.S. Fish and Wildlife Service, 47 p.

Perry, R.W., Skalski, J.R., Brandes, P.L., Sandstrom, P.T., Klimley, A.P., Ammann, A., and MacFarlane, B., 2010, Estimating survival and migration route probabilities of juvenile Chinook salmon in the Sacramento-San Joaquin River Delta: North American Journal of Fisheries Management, v. 30, p. 142–156.

R Development Core Team, 2011, R—A language and environment for statistical computing: Vienna, Austria, R Foundation for Statistical Computing, ISBN 3-900051-07-0, accessed August, 2011, at http://www.r-project.org/.

Seber, G.A.F., 1982, The estimation of animal abundance and related parameters (2d ed.): Caldwell, New Jersey, Blackburn Press, 654 p.

Townsend, R.L., Skalski, J.R., Dillingham, P., and Steig, T.W., 2006, Correcting bias in survival estimation resulting from tag failure in acoustic and radiotelemetry studies: Journal of Agricultural, Biological, and Environmental Statistics, v.11, p. 183–196.

Vogel, D.A., 2010, Evaluation of acoustic-tagged juvenile Chinook salmon movements in the Sacramento-San Joaquin Delta during the 2009 Vernalis Adaptive Management Program: Natural Resource Scientists, Inc., accessed May, 3, 2013, at http://www.sjrg.org/technicalreport/, (2009 VAMP tagged salmon report) 63 p.

Vogel, D.A., 2011, Evaluation of acoustic-tagged juvenile Chinook salmon and predatory fish movements in the Sacramento – San Joaquin Delta during the 2010 Vernalis Adaptive Management Program: Natural Resource Scientists, Inc., accessed May 3, 2013, at *http://www.sjrg.org/technicalreport/*, (2010 Predator tagging study) 72 p.

Williams, J.G., 2006, Central Valley salmon—A perspective on Chinook and steelhead in the Central Valley of California: San Francisco Estuary and Watershed Science, v. 4, no. 3, p. 1–398.

Appendix A

Table A1. Detection probability estimates, with standard error in parentheses, for all releases of acoustically tagged late-fall juvenile Chinook salmon, Sacramento-San Joaquin River Delta, California, winter 2008–09.

[Parameters not estimated are indicated by an "NA" in the estimate column, and parameters fixed at a constant value are noted by an "NA" in parentheses]

Parameter	R_1	R_2	R_3	R_4	R_5	R_6	R_7	R_8	R_9	R_{10}
P_{A2}	0.821 (0.043)	0.571 (0.062)	0.911 (0.042)	0.967 (0.023)	0.990(0.01)	1.000 (NA)	0.977 (0.016)	1.000 (NA)	0.961 (0.022)	0.776 (0.051)
P_{A3}	0.961 (0.038)	1.000 (NA)	1.000 (NA)	1.000 (NA)	0.984 (0.016)	1.000 (NA)	1.000 (NA)	1.000 (NA)	1.000 (NA)	1.000 (NA)
P_{A4}	0.933 (0.065)	1.000 (NA)	1.000 (NA)	0.857 (0.094)	0.962 (0.037)	1.000 (NA)	1.000 (NA)	1.000 (NA)	1.000 (NA)	1.000 (NA)
$P_{A4,Ryd}$	1.000 (NA)	1.000 (NA)	1.000 (NA)	0.909 (0.087)	1.000 (0)	1.000 (NA)	1.000 (NA)	0.962 (0.038)	0.964(0.035)	1.000 (NA)
$P_{A5,Geo}$	1.000 (NA)	0.667 (0.333)	1.000 (NA)	0.926 (0.08)	0.929 (0.074)	0.947 (0.054)	1.000 (NA)	1.000 (NA)	1.000 (NA)	0.952 (0.054)
$P_{A5,Ryd}$	0.889 (0.086)	1.000 (NA)	1.000 (NA)	1.000 (NA)	1.000 (NA)	0.977 (0.024)	1.000 (NA)	1.000 (NA)	1.000 (NA)	1.000 (NA)
$P_{A5,Sac}$	0.889 (0.074)	1.000 (NA)	1.000 (NA)	0.977 (0.025)	1.000 (NA)	0.974 (0.026)	1.000 (NA)	0.992 (0.009)	1.000 (NA)	1.000 (NA)
P_{B11}	1.000 (NA)	0.988 (0.012)	1.000 (NA)	1.000 (NA)	1.000 (NA)	0.964 (0)	1.000 (NA)	1.000 (NA)	1.000 (NA)	1.000 (NA)
P_{B2}	1.000 (NA)	1.000 (NA)	1.000 (NA)	1.000 (NA)	1.000 (NA)	0.9 (0.067)	1.000 (NA)	1.000 (NA)	1.000 (NA)	1.000 (NA)
P_{B21}	1.000 (NA)	0.947 (0.053)	1.000 (NA)	1.000 (NA)	1.000 (NA)	1.000 (NA)	1.000 (NA)	1.000 (NA)	1.000 (NA)	0.995 (0.006)
P_{C1}	0.857 (0.094)	1.000 (NA)	1.000 (NA)	0.857 (0.094)	0.961 (0.038)	1.000 (NA)	0 (0)	NA	NA	NA
P_{C2}	0.720 (0.234)	1.000 (NA)	0.750 (0 153)	1.000 (NA)	0.961 (0.038)	1.000 (NA)	1.000 (NA)	NA	NA	NA
P_{D1}	0.857 (0.094)	1.000 (NA)	1.000 (NA)	0.857 (0.094)	0.961 (0.038)	1.000 (NA)	1.000 (NA)	1.000 (NA)	1.000 (NA)	1.000 (NA)
$P_{D2,Sac}$	0.500 (0.353)	1.000 (NA)	1.000 (NA)	1.000 (NA)	1.000 (NA)	1.000 (NA)	1.000 (NA)	1.000 (NA)	1.000 (NA)	1.000 (NA)
$P_{D2\ Geo}$	1.000 (NA)	0.750 (0.217)	0.875 (0)	0.700 (0.145)	0.846 (0.1)	0.950 (0.049)	1.000 (NA)	1.000 (NA)	1.000 (NA)	0.900 (0.095)

Appendix B

Table B1. Routing probability estimates, with standard error in parentheses, for all releases (R_i) of acoustically tagged late-fall juvenile Chinook salmon, Sacramento-San Joaquin River Delta, California, winter 2008–09.

[Parameter: Open and closed signify the status of the Delta Cross Channel gates. Parameters not estimated are indicated by an "NA" in the estimate column, and parameters fixed at a constant value are noted by an "NA" in parentheses]

Parameter	R_1	R_2	R_3	R_4	R_5	R_6	R_7	R_8	R_9	R_{10}
Ψ_{A1}	0.894 (0.030)	0.678 (0.046)	0.651 (0.049)	0.737 (0.043)	0.712 (0.036)	0.682 (0.039)	0.772 (0.037)	0.695 (0.040)	0.741 (0.040)	0.735 (0.041)
$\Psi_{A2,closed}$	0.651 (0.059)	0.746 (0.057)	0.750 (0.217)	0.641 (0.123)	0.734 (0.045)	0.744 (0.048)	0.718 (0.049)	0.776 (0.048)	0.684 (0.053)	0.701 (0.056)
$\Psi_{A2,open}$	0 333 (0.192)	0.500 (0.250)	0.488 (0.078)	0.611 (0.076)	0.400 (0.219)	0.625 (0.171)	0.000 (NA)	NA	NA	NA
Ψ_{B11}	0.077 (0.026)	0.182 (0.037)	0.254 (0.045)	0.150 (0.035)	0.192 (0.032)	0.198 (0.034)	0.160 (0.032)	0.198 (0.035)	0.059 (0.021)	0.141 (0.032)
Ψ_{B21}	0.029 (0.016)	0.140 (0.034)	0.095 (0.030)	0 113 (0.031)	0.096 (0.024)	0.120 (0.027)	0.069 (0.022)	0.107 (0.027)	0.201 (0.037)	0.124 (0.030)
$\Psi_{C2,open}$	0.667 (0.192)	0.250 (0.217)	0.463 (0.078)	0.136 (0.052)	0.394 (0.218)	0.375 (0.171)	1.000 (NA)	NA	NA	NA
$\Psi_{D2,closed}$	0.349 (0.059)	0.254 (0.057)	0.250 (0.217)	0.359 (0.123)	0.266 (0.045)	0.256 (0.048)	0.282 (0.049)	0.224 (0.048)	0.316 (0.053)	0.299 (0.056)
$\Psi_{D2,open}$	0.000 (NA)	0.250 (0.217)	0.049 (0.034)	0 253 (0.070)	0.206 (0.183)	0.000 (NA)	0.000 (NA)	NA	NA	NA

Appendix C

Table C1. Survival probability estimates, with standard error in parentheses, for all releases (R_i) of acoustically tagged late-fall juvenile Chinook salmon, Sacramento-San Joaquin River Delta, California, winter 2008–09.

[Parameter: Open and closed signify the status of the Delta cross channel gates. Gates were closed for all fish in releases R_8, R_9, and R_{10}. Parameters not estimated are indicated by an "NA" in the estimate column, and parameters fixed at a constant value are noted by an "NA" in parentheses]

Parameter	R_1	R_2	R_3	R_4	R_5	R_6	R_7	R_8	R_9	R_{10}
S_{A1}	0.648 (0.040)	0.634 (0.041)	0.546 (0.039)	0.599 (0.037)	0.830 (0.027)	0.822 (0.029)	0.768 (0.032)	0.757 (0.033)	0.691 (0.035)	0.699 (0.039)
S_{A2}	0.878 (0.049)	0.837 (0.056)	0.732 (0.059)	0.780 (0.052)	0.931 (0.025)	0.928 (0.026)	0.848 (0.036)	0.835 (0.039)	0.859 (0.038)	0.754 (0.052)
$S_{A3,closed}$	0.506 (0.077)	0.477 (0.075)	0.333 (0.272)	0.884 (0.136)	0.865 (0.049)	0.902 (0.038)	0.869 (0.043)	0.780 (0.054)	0.635 (0.067)	0.617 (0.071)
$S_{A3,open}$	1.000 (NA)	0.500 (0.354)	0.650 (0.107)	0.720 (0.107)	1.000 (NA)	0.800 (0.179)	NA	NA	NA	NA
$S_{A3,Ryd}$	0.449 (0.060)	0.304 (0.055)	0.400 (0.061)	0.429 (0.066)	0.783 (0.050)	0.826 (0.046)	0.899 (0.036)	0.799 (0.053)	0.767 (0.054)	0.522 (0.06)
$S_{A4,Sac}$	0.588 (0.122)	0.682 (0.099)	0.143 (0.094)	0.491 (0.103)	0.388 (0.062)	0.609 (0.068)	0.377 (0.067)	0.680 (0.070)	0.545 (0.087)	0.552 (0.092)
$S_{A4,Ryd}$	0.435 (0.107)	0.048 (0.046)	0.154 (0.071)	0.333 (0.086)	0.389 (0.066)	0.449 (0.068)	0.226 (0.053)	0.472 (0.069)	0.529 (0.070)	0.306 (0.077)
S_{B11}	0.125 (0.117)	0.198 (0.089)	0.208 (0.083)	0.438 (0.124)	0.567 (0.09)	0.815 (0.087)	0.476 (0.109)	0.769 (0.083)	0.571 (0.187)	0.353 (0.116)
S_{B21}	0.333 (0.272)	0.387 (0.126)	0.556 (0.166)	0.583 (0.142)	0.800 (0.103)	0.738 (0.118)	0.556 (0.166)	0.643 (0.128)	0.667 (0.096)	0.799 (0.104)
S_{B3}	0.562 (0.400)	0.200 (0.126)	0.500 (0.158)	0.438 (0.136)	0.517 (0.093)	0.577 (0.091)	0.267 (0.114)	0.522 (0.094)	0.750 (0.097)	0.500 (0.118)
S_{C1}	1.000 (NA)	1.000 (NA)	0.842 (0.148)	1.000 (NA)	1.000 (NA)	1.000 (NA)	1.000 (NA)	NA	NA	NA
S_{C2}	0.000 (NA)	1.000 (NA)	0.500 (0.144)	0.500 (0.204)	0.500 (0.353)	0.667 (0.272)	0.000 (NA)	NA	NA	NA
$S_{D1,Sac,closed}$	0.764 (0.523)	0.400 (0.126)	1.000 (NA)	0.432 (0.220)	0.801 (0.080)	0.810 (0.086)	0.500 (0.102)	0.706 (0.111)	0.458 (0.102)	0.600 (0.11)
$S_{D1,Geo}$	0.228 (0.042)	0.259 (0.081)	0.095 (0.032)	0.261 (0.059)	0.416 (0.063)	0.614 (0.054)	0.574 (0.048)	0.541 (0.048)	0.458 (0.048)	0.335 (0.055)
$S_{D1,Sac,open}$	1.000 (NA)	1.000 (NA)	0.000 (NA)	0.478 (0.162)	1.000 (NA)	0.000 (NA)	0.000 (NA)	NA	NA	NA
$S_{D2,Sac}$	0.113 (0.107)	0.125 (0.117)	0.111 (0.105)	0.372 (0.149)	0.304 (0.096)	0.270 (0.104)	0.417 (0.142)	0.588 (0.144)	0.455 (0.150)	0.167 (0.108)
$S_{D2,Geo}$	0.130 (0.070)	0.225 (0.164)	0.111 (0.106)	0.302 (0.100)	0.312 (0.083)	0.318 (0.064)	0.274 (0.057)	0.271 (0.058)	0.347 (0.068)	0.295 (0.085)
ω_{open}	0.077 (0.030)	0.063 (0.031)	0.911 (0.042)	0.720 (0.060)	0.049 (0.021)	0.089 (0.030)	0.012 (0.012)	NA	NA	NA

Appendix D

Files of release-specific capture histories and model likelihoods for program USER were included as a separate attachment to this report.

36

www.ingramcontent.com/pod-product-compliance
Lightning Source LLC
Chambersburg PA
CBHW080347290526
45791CB00009BA/2777